A *WESTERN HORSEMAN* BOOK

RIDE THE JOURNEY

A Step-by-Step Guide to Authentic Horsemanship

By Chris Cox With Cynthia McFarland

Edited by
Fran Devereux Smith and Cathy Martindale

Photography by
John Brasseaux

Ride The Journey

Published by
WESTERN HORSEMAN magazine
3850 North Nevada Ave.
Box 7980
Colorado Springs, CO 80933-7980
800-877-5278

www.westernhorseman.com

Design, Typography, and Production
Western Horseman
Fort Worth, Texas

Front and Back Cover Photos By
David Stoecklein

Printing
Branch Smith
Fort Worth, Texas

©2008 MCC Magazines, LLC. All Rights Reserved.

*This book is protected by federal copyright law. No material may be
copied, faxed, electronically transmitted, reproduced or otherwise
used without express written permission. Requests must
be submitted in writing to* **Western Horseman**.

Manufactured in the United States of America

First Printing: April 2008

ISBN 978-0-911647-82-2

WESTERN HORSEMAN is a registered trademark of MCC Magazines, LLC.

DEDICATION AND ACKNOWLEDGMENTS

My life has been built on dreams; as a child I dreamed every day. God has helped me answer most of those dreams. I could never have been blessed with the ability and talent to work with horses, or to speak in front of thousands of people, without Him being beside me.

Thanks to Lee Reborse for bringing his horsemanship to Australia in the 1970s, and to Ken May for laying a great foundation in passing along Lee's teaching of the horse.

To my Rancheros Vistadores family, your friendship has changed my life.

To Jim and Mary Pruett, for the love and support you've given me over the years, in failure and success.

To my brother Gene, for being a great cowboy, husband, and father to your children.

To my brother Lamar, for being so hard on me growing up, which has taken me most of my life to overcome, but at the same time has helped me become stronger and more determined to overcome the obstacles life puts in front of me.

To Papa (Dad), for shipping us to the end of the world and making horses and cattle our lives.

To Momma, for your belief in me and your positive attitude.

To Cynthia McFarland, thank you for your friendship through the years, for helping me to get my thoughts on paper and for making this book a success.

To all the horse owners who believe in the message of my horsemanship, I value your friendship and support. This book is for all of you.

CONTENTS

FOREWORD

To Chris Cox,

You're a great teller of jokes, as evidenced by your expertise during the Rancheros Vistadores' gatherings. So when you asked me to write the foreword to your book, my initial response was the one my old friend Frankie Emmerling, owner of a Denver, Colo., steakhouse, gave when a patron asked him to autograph her napkin.

"I am honored to have been asked to write
   in your album;
I hardly know where to begin!
The only original thing about me...
Is the stain of original sin!"

You appreciated Frankie's humor as much as I did, and you still wanted to include my thoughts in your book. So, here's to you, Chris!

To the Readers,

My introduction to Chris Cox came when my friend Billy Minnick called and needed an "unstarted 2-year-old" for a Chris Cox demonstration at Billy Bob's Texas, where a group of businessmen from China were getting a Cowtown welcome. I took a little red roan filly—and I lied about her age. She really was 3 years old, but that didn't seem to make any difference to Chris!

I was instantly in awe of his athletic ability, his impeccable timing and the feel that he had with the horse. I also instantly sensed that I was witnessing a young superstar. With these horses, it's all about developing more knowledge, and Chris Cox has the knowledge everyone should be exposed to. I always thought that to become a master it required years and years of experience, but Chris proved me wrong as he has incredible knowledge beyond his years.

For a humble and egoless man such as me, what I've just said about Chris is right on. This young man, Chris Cox, has integrity and total dedication, and, as a result, an intensity seldom seen. The combination has made him a true champion for the horse and people who love the horse. Chris is the real deal, he is authentic, and he truly is a master horseman.

Larry Mahan
Six-time World Champion All-Around Cowboy
(Professional) Rodeo Cowboys Association

DARRELL DODDS

INTRODUCTION

Horsemanship is a way of life and an exciting journey. Along the way you discover the journey is not just about the horse; the journey is about you, as well. It's about getting to know yourself and learning to control your emotions so that you can communicate clearly with this wonderful animal, the horse. Always keep an open mind and never lose your passion, and you'll never lose the direction for your journey.

Knowledge is power. The more knowledge and understanding you have, the more effective you can be in communicating to your horse, as well as to others in your life. I encourage you to walk through your horsemanship journey in steps and to complete each step several times before moving to the next level. Once you connect with your horse and your communication is effective, your horse starts trying to please you and looks to you for guidance. That's when your partnership really starts to come alive. When you experience this kind of partnership, it stays with you and inspires you for the rest of your life.

I hope those of you already involved in this lifestyle will continue to advance and learn about your horses, and that those of you just getting into horses will be safe and not become frustrated. Either way, having a system and a program can help guide you step-by-step through a wonderful lifestyle. My wish for each of you is that you gain many wonderful experiences and fulfill your dreams through this amazing journey with the horses in your life.

God bless you, your family, and the horses you ride,

Chris Cox

"Horses have fascinated me as long as I can remember, and the more time I spent with them, the more I was drawn to understand them better."

1

HORSEMAN IN THE MAKING

The truth is that I can't remember my first time on a horse. Old photos in family albums and scrapbooks show me perched on a horse before I was 18 months old; I was riding before I was walking. Being around horses has been as natural to me as breathing for as long as I can remember. The feel of horses, their presence and my relationship with them has defined my life. Horses have always been, and remain, in large part responsible for the man I am today.

Born into a ranching family in Kissimmee, Fla., all of my earliest memories included horses. Horses, cattle and ranching were in my blood. I realized early on this wasn't something you *did;* it was who you *were.* My parents, Edward Eugene "Gene" and Aileene Cox, were proud of the family's ranching background

The Road to the Horse is a great event, and I was privileged to be there. (Chris followed his 2007 win with another win in 2008.)

and raised their sons, Lamar, Gene and me, to follow in that tradition.

My mother's family hails from Tennessee, while my father was raised in Kissimmee, Fla., and Georgia. His own father died young, so the grandfather for whom my father was named, Edward Eugene Cox, mainly raised my dad. That grandfather was a judge and also a Georgia congressman for 20-plus years, and because of this, my dad spent a lot of time at the White House in Washington, D.C., while he was growing up. Also through his grandfather's connections in the U.S. Congress, my father, while still a young boy, was introduced to his grandfather's close friend, Richard Mifflin "Dick" Kleberg Sr.

Richard Kleberg was a seven-term Texas congressman, but more important to my dad was the fact that the Kleberg family owned the historic King Ranch in Texas. Kleberg's father had married Alice, the youngest daughter of King Ranch founder, Richard King, and later worked with King's widow, Henrietta, to continue consolidating and developing the ranch's massive holdings.

Kleberg welcomed his friend's grandson, and my dad spent his childhood summers on the King Ranch. His experiences there made a huge impression on my father, and by the time he was in his 20s, he had bought his own ranch in his hometown of Kissimmee. My family owned ranchland in that area of central Florida before Walt Disney came along and turned it into a tourist mecca.

Australia Beckons

My dad always looked for adventure and wide-open country. Before I was even born, he had gone to Australia, where he found work on large ranches in the country's northeastern region. During that time, my dad met a gentleman named Jimmy Joyce, who owned an entire island, the largest in the area. Prince of Wales Island was 100 square miles of pasture and woods surrounded by ocean. To my father, it was heaven.

He returned to Florida, where I was born in 1967, but he couldn't shake loose the idea of that island ranchland. My dad loved ranch-

My brothers, (from left) Gene and Lamar, and I grew up "down under" on Prince of Wales Island, 100 square miles of pasture and woods.

Horses were the primary island transportation for my family, which included (from left) my mother, Aileene Cox; my great-grandmother, Flora J. Batey, who was 98 when the photo was taken; my father Gene; and we three boys, Lamar (at left), Gene (center), and me.

As a youngster, I competed in Pony Club and campdrafting, which is similar to the working cow horse event.

Cattle bought to improve the Cox family herd were off-loaded from the ship into the sea, where they swam to Prince of Wales Island.

As a teenager I rode bulls for a while, but always realized horsemanship was the career I would pursue.

ing and raising cattle, and it didn't take long for him to decide that Australia offered more future opportunity than Florida could provide at the time.

That settled, he bought the island from Jimmy Joyce. He and my mom packed up everything and everyone—including my then 96-year-old great-grandmother, Flora J. Batey, from Orlando—and we moved "down under" when I was not much more than a year old.

Growing up on that island, everything in my childhood revolved around horses and cattle. The only transportation on the island was our horses and a Massey Ferguson tractor, so every day, no matter where we went, we boys rode horses.

At first, my mother home-schooled my two older brothers and me, but by the time I was ready for second grade, our parents had decided we should attend public school on Thursday Island. So we rode our horses to the front beach, put them in a corral for the day, and then took a boat to the island for school. Afterward, we rode our horses home.

The passion for horses that drives me today started very early in life, so early that I can't really put a finger on when I first felt it. I only know that horses have fascinated me as long as I can remember, and the more time I spent with them, the more I was drawn to understand them better.

My first horse was an old Australian Brumby horse named Major; I got him after we moved to the island. He knew every inch of that land, and he could be stubborn at times, but he had a very expressive personality. Major also could be tough to catch, so I had to learn to think like he did, and this, in turn, drove me to want to figure out better ways to communicate with horses in general, and Major in particular.

My brothers and I competed in Pony Club and also in campdrafting, which is similar to the working cow horse event. We rode Australian saddles and also western stock saddles my family had brought from the United States.

My parents' chosen career put livestock at the center of my life, but I can't honestly say I inherited my passion for horses from either of them. My mother rode, but she wasn't really into horses; she worked long days taking care of my family and always cooked for the ranch hands. My father was a saltwater cowboy, who could ride and get the job done with the best of them, but he was all about using the horse

as a tool to work cattle. While still in elementary school, I realized that my father and I looked at horses differently. To my dad, the horse was a means to an end, little more than a tool. I was already discovering that I could become partners with a horse.

"I learned firsthand that I could replace the fear with knowledge."

Early Mentors

When I was about 10 years old, I attended a clinic at Charters Tower, North Queensland, and met my first master horseman, Lee Reborse. Originally from Nevada, Lee, like my father, had been drawn to the opportunities available in Australia. Lee actually is responsible for refining much of the horsemanship in Australia today. He had a lot of the skills I wanted to develop, and he was a great teacher. Even better, he was a great communicator with his horses, which motivated my passion all the more. Watching Lee, I knew that if I could become more skillful, then I would become more effective with horses. That, more than anything, was what I wanted.

Another strong influence in my life was Charlie Edgar, a horseman who worked for my dad. I gathered cattle with Charlie, and he was a positive influence on me and my horsemanship at an early age.

About this same time my family moved from the island to the mainland, which opened more doors to me. During the summers and school breaks, I could sign on with big outfits to help muster, or gather, their cattle. There were times when we contracted to muster a million-acre ranch. For a kid like me, that was a dream come true. The ranch owner allotted each rider a couple of horses to work, and after working so closely together every day, I created real bonds with mine.

After two or three months, when we'd leave to go to the next ranch, I really missed those horses and the partnerships we shared. These were working horses—nothing fancy or highly bred—but each horse and I really had become a team as we worked to gather cattle. When I had that bond with a horse, the horse

Mineral Wells, Texas, is a fine place to call home. I moved there in late 1999, and built the Diamond Double C Ranch, which is headquarters for Chris Cox Horsemanship Company.

actually would look after me. In fact, ranch owners and other riders often noticed and commented on how well my horses worked.

I think a certain bond can come only from passion, and I also think that passion can be nurtured and developed. Drawn to horses from my earliest memories, I believe I developed that passion by working with them.

In my early teens, I started many young horses. Naturally I couldn't stick on each of those horses every time, and I bucked off some. I built a healthy amount of fear, but quickly realized that if I didn't overcome the fear, it would ruin my passion for horses. I learned firsthand that I could replace the fear with knowledge. When I was better prepared and my techniques became smoother, the horses responded better. As I got on more and more horses, I made it a point to learn to read their responses, to try to anticipate what they might do before they did it. The more I rode, the more I learned. The process was addictive.

As a teenager, I rode bulls for a while and earned the money to pay my entry fees by working on ranches and starting colts. I soon realized I didn't want a career as a rodeo cowboy. But I always knew horses would be a permanent part of my life—they were the backbone behind everything I did.

I went to boarding school as a teen and hated it. Every chance I had, I stole away to help muster cattle. After graduation, I attended Longreach Agricultural College in Queensland, a two-year college. Ken May, a horsemanship instructor there and one of Lee Reborse's students, was a very positive influence on me. I respected Ken's horsemanship, and we developed a friendship along the way. At the time, I scored the highest horsemanship marks of any student and also won the school's horsemanship award. During college and for a short time after, I helped Ken conduct colt-starting and horsemanship clinics.

Heading to America

In Australia, a person is judged by the horse he rides. I learned to think of that as letting my horse be my promotion. A person can talk all day long about what he can do with a horse, but in the end the horse shows the kind of rider a person is—or isn't.

I gained a huge amount of respect for the talented horsemen and horsewomen I had met, but, as much as I loved growing up in

I've spent so many hours horseback, working for my dad and for other ranchers, and that experience was a great teacher.

Australia and all my experiences there, I'd always dreamed of coming back to the States. I knew if I was to make a career with horses, my best opportunity would be in the United States. By 1986, I'd saved enough money to buy a ticket, and I flew back to Florida.

I landed in Kissimmee, not far from where I was born, and headed to the ranch of old family friends, the Overstreets. As it turned out, they were getting ready to work cows, which was fine by me after being on a plane for so long. The very next day found me horseback, helping gather 5,000 head of cattle.

As much as I enjoyed cowboying and working with cattle, I knew I wanted to focus on horses. After staying with my friends a few days, I went to visit some of my mother's relatives in Tennessee. While there, I met some neighbors, who had a 3-year-old Tennessee Walking Horse filly they couldn't ride. She lit-

The Diamond Double C Ranch is in the heart of Texas cutting-horse country.

The diamond-double-C is becoming a well-recognized brand.

erally bucked off the saddle. They bet me $300 that I couldn't saddle and ride her. I was hungry at the time, so I took the challenge; I started that filly and rode her within an hour. That was my first "clinic" in the United States.

I wanted to work for a trainer, so I found work in Texas with John Carter, who trained cutting horses. From the beginning, I've always loved cutting horses. I really appreciate the athletic ability and smarts of a good cow horse. Growing up on a ranch made me believe a horse must have a job, and I still believe this. A horse must have a purpose, and that can't be only going around and around an arena.

After working for John Carter a year, I decided I was ready to give it a go on my own; I was 19 years old at the time. I rented a facility in Madisonville, Texas, where I started colts and cutting horses, and I also began doing some demonstrations and clinics.

Building a Career

Later, while renting a facility in Geneva, Ala., I first started offering clinics at my place. A short time later, I moved back to Florida—this time to the Panhandle—and rented another training operation. Then I got one of my first big breaks as a clinician. I had started a mustang at one of my clinics, and somehow word of this had reached a Bureau of Land Management employee. BLM got in touch with me and, after seeing my work, contracted with me to go to adoption sites in different states and demonstrate how to start these newly captured mustangs.

Back in the late 1980s and early 1990s, it was very difficult to make a full-time living conducting clinics. So while I did BLM demonstrations, I also trained outside horses at my rented facility, as well as some cutting horses for various owners. My first training video, *Breaking into the Horse's Mind*, was released in 1990.

After years of renting training operations, I was more than ready to own a place, and in 1995 bought my first ranch in Ocala, Fla. Ocala, in Marion County, is widely known as "Horse Capital of the World," thanks to the huge numbers of champions and producers of many breed champions there. When I go back to Florida for clinics and tour stops, in a way it's like coming home. My introduction to horses started there, and I still have friends and family in the state.

People sometimes have a hard time thinking of ranching when they think of Florida. Thanks to television and very successful advertising on the part of tourist attractions, most people's ideas of the state involve beaches, palm trees and Mickey Mouse. Yet, agriculture is a major industry in Florida, second only to tourism. Thousands of acres still are devoted to ranching and raising horses and cattle. The challenging terrain and conditions are the reasons early Florida cowpunchers were called "Crackers." They earned the title by cracking their whips as they drove headstrong cattle out of treacherous bogs, woods and dense brush too thick to ride through horseback.

Rodeo also is big in Florida. Sunshine State cowboys and cowgirls ride, rope, spin and cut their way into the big money at competitions around the country, including the National Finals Rodeo. Florida was a great place to get my career really moving, but when I had the opportunity to buy raw land in Texas and build my own place from the ground up exactly the way I wanted, I jumped on it.

I've always felt a strong bond with the state of Texas. In addition to my father's King Ranch connections, one of my ancestors was Mirabeau Buonaparte Lamar. Born in Georgia in 1798, he moved to Texas in 1835 and joined the Texas revolutionary army under General Sam Houston. Lamar became president of the Republic of Texas from 1838 to 1841. An expert horseman, he is considered the "Father of Texas Education," with many schools across the state named for him. My oldest brother, Lamar, is named in his honor, as well.

I moved to Mineral Wells, Texas, in late 1999, and I'm there to stay. This area also is serious horse country, and not far from the "Cutting Horse Capital" of Weatherford. Mineral Wells is a fine place to call home, and I've built a great facility there for teaching my weeklong courses, as well as for training young horses.

Although my parents and I live on different continents, they have been extremely supportive of my career. My dad still ranches in Australia, and both my brothers make their livings by cowboying and starting horses. I respect what they do with horses and am grateful for everything I learned from them. My own goals with horses are different from theirs, but that doesn't take anything away from their own knowledge and vast experience.

I spent so many hours on the back of a horse when I was working with my dad and for other ranchers, and that experience was a great teacher. Learning rhythm, learning the

"A good horseman has to acknowledge that tough horses often are the best teachers."

intricacies of a horse's footfall, watching how the horse responds—so many of those things I took for granted because they were part of my everyday life. I realize now how fortunate I was, because not everyone gets to spend so much time in the saddle early in life.

I've learned a lot of things the hard way, and I have certainly struggled with many horses while getting that education. A good horseman has to acknowledge that tough horses often are the best teachers. To learn and keep on learning, a horseman must be willing to admit when he's wrong and that he doesn't have all the answers. When it comes to horses, I haven't always done things the right way or the easiest way, but I've always been determined to learn better ways.

Through the years, I've been around a lot of people who manhandle their horses. I've also seen many people, even professional trainers, who use a "cookie cutter" application with every horse, but horses don't work that way. Horses are individuals with their own minds and emotions. I think we have to acknowledge this before we can get anywhere with any horse. Once I began to understand the horse's mind, I had a much clearer direction about the methods I needed to apply to accomplish what I wanted to do with my horses.

As horsemen, we never finish learning. I'll never totally understand all the mysteries of the horse, but I've made it my journey in life to keep peeling back the layers, to continue discovering more and more about the horse's mind and what he is telling me.

"The difference between a horseman and a trainer is that the trainer trains the horse while the horseman trains himself."

2

PUT THEORY INTO PRACTICE

Through many years, my experiences with horses—both positive and negative—have helped me develop the training methods that I use today. From a very early age, I was fortunate to spend most of my time riding and working with horses, and I believe the horse has been my greatest teacher.

We all can learn valuable, life-changing lessons from horses, if only we pay attention. In working with horses, we must be willing to let go of our own agendas at times, and this is tough for many people to swallow. We have to admit that we're not always right. So often, we expect horses to accept what they are asked to do without considering how the horses view such situations. If we don't understand how horses think and we don't work with the

We must never make the mistake of thinking a horse can't communicate.

Pinned ears denote aggression and dominance.

The proverbial soft-eyed horse is considered a desirable riding partner.

horses' minds, we find plenty of roadblocks and battles that can be avoided—if we only learn to "read" our horses.

My horsemanship has been—and still is—an ongoing journey. I always make it a point to keep the horse's needs first and foremost. More than any techniques, it's the philosophy behind everything I do, and it's my understanding of how the horse's mind works that gives me success. I always say that the difference between a horseman and a trainer is that the trainer trains the horse while the horseman trains himself.

So many people, even professionals, miss a lot of cues about what horses, through their body language, are trying to tell their handlers. Such people never have learned to read horses. Unlike humans, horses are fairly transparent; they always "say" what they mean.

Although horses communicate nonverbally, we must never make the mistake of thinking they don't communicate. That is why it's so important to learn to read the horse's body language. He communicates through his expression and body language. A horse never yells a verbal message; some people might wait for that, but it won't happen. Instead, we must learn how to interpret his body language. The good thing: There's a wealth of information available about the psychology of horses and how they think. Through articles, books, television, videos, DVDs, clinics and courses, horse owners today have the best opportunities ever to understand their horses and build great relationships with them.

Read Body Language

Here's what to look for as you learn to read your horse's body language. These different forms of body language tell you about your horse's frame of mind.

- Pay close attention to your horse's eyes and ears. They clue you in to what your horse is thinking and where his attention is focused. Your horse's mind is always directed wherever his ears and eyes are focused.

- Your horse's eyes and ears always tell you when his feet are about to move. His eyes give the first signs that his feet are going to move, then his ears and then his body, and those signs finally transfer down through the body to his feet. If you miss the signs in the eyes and ears, you can find them in the body as your horse moves forward, kicks, bucks, etc. Some horses react faster than others, but this always is the pattern.

- Licking his lips means your horse is relaxed. This always is a positive sign.

- When your horse turns away and swings his hindquarters toward you, he is either dismissing you or threatening you, or he's afraid of something.

- When your horse's ears flick back and forth, he might be confused and sorting out things, or trying to take in everything happening around him.

- Ears that are flat back denote aggression or dominance.

- A stiff neck and head carriage indicate your horse might be frightened, or he could be showing aggression or resistance.

- A horse that feels threatened or cornered usually reacts in a flighty manner. He also might act "bullish" and have little forward motion. If he feels too much pressure, he might retaliate by kicking, striking, pawing or biting. This seldom happens, but can occur when a stallion doesn't think he has a way out of the situation.

- A frightened horse goes into survival mode. He adopts submissive body language and might actually quiver. He also might exhibit a lot of forward motion because he's looking for a way out of the situation. He doesn't want to challenge you, but still can present a danger because his entire focus is on getting away from whatever he views as frightening.

- A "sour" horse has had all he can take and reveals his attitude through his body language. He might fling his head and swish his tail, but his body is stiff, and he also has a "sharp" look to his eye.

Purpose and Communication

Any time your horse changes his mind and, thus, his thought process, it is apparent through

This horse's ears are attuned to whatever is behind him; consequently, that's where his attention is directed.

With one ear forward and one to the side, this horse's attention is divided; he might be trying to figure out what's happening around him.

This horse's attention is focused on what's straight ahead, according to his ear position.

his body language. He might resist and become stiff, or yield and become soft and willing. If his body language is resistant, it's up to you to react immediately before that resistant thinking transfers to his feet and into movement.

Ponying another horse is just one of the many jobs a riding horse can have.

As horsemen and -women, we're not perfect, and we make mistakes. Whenever we do something wrong horseback, we should try to correct it immediately—before it transfers into movement on the horse's part.

Your horse must think about something before he does it, and you can use this to your advantage. When your horse thinks about doing something negative, such as bucking, rearing or running off, he signals you first. If you pay attention to his body language, you have a chance to redirect him in a positive way.

You must train yourself to communicate clearly to your horse through your own body language. It takes time to develop your instincts around horses so that your responses to your horse's actions literally become second nature.

I don't have to think about my responses as much as I did early in my riding career, but I never want to stop being aware. Awareness keeps me in tune with my horse's actions and thought processes. When I take what my horse does for granted, I might lose momentum going forward with his training, or even get myself hurt.

There should be a reason for anything I do with a horse—on the ground or in the saddle. I don't believe in doing something with a horse if what I do has no specific meaning or purpose. The reason: When a horse doesn't find purpose in what he's asked to do, he eventually becomes sour or develops a bad attitude; he loses his incentive and motive.

That's why you must inspire your horse, and the way to do this is by helping him achieve things that make sense to him. You don't want to take your horse's natural instinct from him because this instinct actually helps him learn.

Horses are very purposeful animals. Whether they walk across a pasture to water or maneuver to find the sweetest grazing or the best shady spot, there is a reason behind what they do. Horses obviously are practical animals, and we can learn plenty from them about practicality and purpose. Remember: The horse is a purposeful animal, period. That's why your horsemanship must be purposeful.

That's why you give your horse a job to do, even if it's just going on a trail ride, trailing a cow, or riding to the mailbox. When your horse understands what you ask him to do—whether it's taking a jump, crossing a creek, or working a cow—he tries harder when he finds purpose in that action. Every time you work with a horse, use techniques and applications to set up things so that your horse can please you. Look for him to make that effort. When you have a horse that puts his heart and soul into trying to please you and to do everything he can for you, you know you have a real partner.

People often have the misconception that, because they care for horses, the horses will be their friends. I'm sometimes asked if I consider my horses to be my friends. I do, but not in the way the person asking might think.

"Horses learn through relief from pressure. Relief of that pressure is critical to successful training."

Friendship between a horse and a human isn't equal. The human must be the leader if the partnership is to be effective. So you must be the leader, and your horse must be a follower. If your leadership skills are smooth and authoritative in ways he understands, he actually is happy to follow your lead. Your horse can and should feel comfortable around you. He shouldn't feel threatened or intimidated, but always should know that you are in charge. You must demonstrate leadership skills to direct your horse's thought processes and emotions, which transfer into his actions. Your horse must look to you for confidence, support and leadership.

When you approach a horse that hasn't been handled, or has been handled in the wrong ways, the first thing in his mind is to protect himself. "How can I stay safe?" runs through his mind.

I guarantee you: He's not thinking, "Hey, maybe I can make friends with this person."

In fact, most of the time that horse reverts to the easiest response, which simply is to flee. Confining or roping that horse can put him into panic mode. Instead, you must start developing the horse's trust by using rhythm, feel and timing as you work to build the horse's confidence. The better your techniques and skills, the more quickly you can teach your horse.

Think about the differences between a timid, anxious driver and a confident, experienced driver. Both can hop in a car and get to the store, but it takes longer and is a lot more stressful for the timid driver, who lacks a good feel for his task. That is why I always talk about rhythm, feel and timing with horses, which is covered in depth in upcoming chapters.

The Hunt for Relief

Any time you train a horse, pressure plays a key role. It can be pressure from your leg, hand, rein or spur. It also can be pressure from your presence, which your horse picks up on through your body lan-

> *"Once the horse knows that relief comes from you, he always looks to you for relief."*

guage and expression, even when you aren't touching him.

Horses learn through relief from pressure. Relief of that pressure is critical to successful training. The secret is in knowing when to give that relief so the horse learns in a positive way. Once a horse knows the relief comes from you, he always looks to you for relief.

Look at a horse with the bad habit of rearing. Maybe his rider has too strong a bit; maybe that rider is too heavy-handed. In this example, the "why" doesn't matter as much as the "what." When the horse rears—whether he tries to avoid the bit, the rider's hands, or both—the rider loosens the reins and grabs the horn to stay in the saddle. The horse soon learns that when he rears, the pressure immediately goes away. Because relief comes when he rears, you can bet he keeps doing that until and unless someone can show him how to find relief in another way.

The gift of relief is the greatest gift you can give your horse. In his mind this is better than praise, petting or treats. This is why you always make sure that you give your horse a

Obviously this horse, dismayed by the pressure created from being tied, hasn't figured out how to give to that pressure and find relief.

clear pathway in the direction you want him to go; then he can find that relief.

It's very important to set up a training situation so that the horse can find his own answers. I think of it as setting up perimeters, or establishing boundaries that allow the horse to find that relief. If I want a horse to give to my hands, for example, I don't tug and pull on his head. Pulling creates only resistance. Instead, I hold my hands still in one place until the horse gives to the pressure. As soon as he does, I immediately release my hands so he has the relief he's hunting. This is what I mean by establishing boundaries for the horse. I don't pull him into position, but I do make it easy for him to find the desired position I want him to take. Relief of pressure is how the horse learns.

Don't do all the learning for your horse by telling him what to do every second. If you do, your horse never has confidence and relies on you too much. Instead, set up a situation so that your horse wants to look for the answers, to hunt for the relief, because this helps him start thinking. Set the boundaries by using your legs, seat and hands, and allow your horse to find the answers by seeking relief from the pressure of those boundaries. Your horse wants to do the least amount of work he has to, which is why you want to set up things for him to succeed.

When you work with a young horse, you must build a foundation in the beginning. But as the horse continues to learn, you should expect him to use what he already knows from that foundation and to begin making decisions for himself by seeking relief. Don't always "spoon-feed" the answers to your horse.

When you handle the relief of pressure the correct way, you can develop total softness in the horse, not just some give or softness. You want this to become your horse's thought process: He does what you ask because he uses the boundaries you have set to find answers (about how to proceed) and make his decisions. If you encourage this willingness and make it the horse's idea to give a response, then he becomes soft in his mind, as well as his body, and that is crucial to horsemanship.

All a horse really wants is relief. Even when you see a horse run away, ultimately it's because he wants relief to do what he wants, whether that's grazing or just relaxing. Horses are like us in this regard. Just ask people what they'd do if they won the lottery, and most will say, "Go on vacation and relax!"

They don't say, "Why, I think I'll just work harder."

Why do we appreciate vacation time? Because it's a break from work, from routine. In the same way, the relief of pressure is a "mini-vacation" for the horse. It's an immediate way to freshen his mind and let him absorb what he's done. Horses like routine. They also like to do things the easy way. That's not a character flaw; it's just the way horses are wired. Through time, as your horse

During a tour stop, a tour participant's horse initially resists giving to pressure on the reins.

Just minutes later, the horse is no longer resisting and is on his way to finding relief, although he has not yet achieved his natural head-set.

Cattle work creates the opportunity to apply training maneuvers in practical ways that make sense to the horse.

grows accustomed to what you ask him to do, he starts looking for a way out, or a shortcut. He starts to anticipate, and that actually can be a good thing, if you handle it correctly.

For example, a person always tries to get a horse to stand still when, instead, the rider could utilize his horse's movement and put his mind and body to work. When a horse doesn't stand still when I've asked, I seize that opportunity to build on techniques and exercises that increase his suppleness.

Movement always is an advantage for accomplishing tasks. So if your horse doesn't want to stand, ask him to do various maneuvers. Keep your horse moving and don't let him stop until it's your idea. If you do this a few times, the next time you drop your reins and ask the horse to stand, he understands that he's supposed to relax and take a breather, so he can prepare for the next job whenever you ask.

"Feel"

When I explain the concept of "feel" to students at my courses, I want them to understand this: Feel is applying the pressure you use to set boundaries with your horse and knowing when to release that pressure.

Developing feel takes time and practice, but you can perfect your feel so that you release pressure the moment the horse gives to you. You might be applying leg pressure as you ask the horse to side-pass, or holding a brace with your rein, asking him to give laterally. In either case, you want to maintain consistency in setting that boundary until your horse gives. As soon as you feel that softening, that give, from your horse, you must release the pressure.

If I lead a horse and he pulls against the lead rope, I maintain my hold with constant pressure. I don't jerk or pull against the horse. That only gives him something to fight against, and fighting never should be the goal with a horse.

Your goal is to remain the constant in the equation. Things might happen all around you, but when your horse knows you are consistent in what you do, he looks to you for leadership. The better your feel becomes, the more in time and rhythm with your horse you are, the smoother things flow between the two of you. Your horse also is better able to understand what you ask of him.

"Soaking"

As you work with your horse, one tool you can use to help him learn is what I call "soaking." This just means that when you get a correct response, you give the horse relief and leave him alone so that he can relax and absorb what he's just learned. A soaking session might last two minutes or 10, depending on the situation.

As this young horse "soaks" to absorb a recent trailer-loading experience, he licks his lips and works his mouth, relaxed and comfortable with the situation.

Only a tremendous amount of trust allows the horse to mirror my movements.

Trust is the key factor in a successful relationship anyone builds with a horse he handles and rides.

During your training sessions, once your horse understands the lesson, and softens and gives when you ask him to perform, stop everything and let your horse soak. Let his mind and body relax so he can take in and register what he's just done right. When a horse relaxes, he usually salivates and licks his lips.

The soaking session is the opposite of what many people think; soaking is not just a "time out." A horse initially learns from a soaking session because he looks forward to the reward of being left alone. Then, when the horse comes back into the training process, he's even better because the soaking gave him time to think without pressure.

Put yourself in your horse's shoes. Soaking is like getting up from your desk and walking outside for a few minutes of fresh air. You certainly don't forget what you were just doing, but the break is a chance to take a deep breath for a moment before you go back to work.

If you use soaking sessions throughout your horse training, you find that they have a much more positive effect than pounding your horse constantly with schooling. By continually pounding away at him, you might get your horse to accept instruction physically, but not mentally. Without that mental acceptance, he eventually starts to resist and challenge you.

It all comes down to how much you teach your horse in increments. With enough soaking time between lessons, you can teach a horse a great deal in only a day.

Establish Trust

There are no shortcuts to building trust with a horse. The only way to establish trust is by working with him and being consistent in what you do. Your horse wants to know that you are consistent. He also tests you to see if you remain consistent and follow through when you ask him to perform.

Horses don't like change; they're creatures of habit. This doesn't mean that you shouldn't change as you improve your skills. But as you advance in your horsemanship, you should build on the basic techniques that you've learned and that your horse understands. Change then becomes a process, so that your horse can transition and improve with you.

I see the need for consistently building on the foundation all the time, especially when a person at one of my courses has a horse someone else has trained. That horse resists making any changes unless the rider first builds on the foundation in increments, which allows the horse to establish trust and confidence in his handler.

Remember: A horse has a very high survival instinct, and this instinct always is there. That awareness and sense of self-preservation make him the way he is.

Practically Speaking: Your Working Pace

Many people work at only one speed around their horses—usually slow. That's because the person's energy level is below his horse's energy level. When that happens, the horse can become spooky when his handler moves quickly.

I want a horse to accept my presence, whether I move slowly or quickly around him, and no matter if I'm on the ground or in the saddle. Such movement actually can comfort a nervous horse. For example, I might ride a young colt that jumps when I touch his rump with my hand. Instead of taking away my hand, I keep touching and rubbing his rump until I get the responses I want—acceptance and relaxed body language.

You need to bring your energy level up to or above that of your horse. When you do, his energy level starts to lower. Raise your energy first, and your horse won't feel the need to raise his. Your energy level shows the horse your confidence, which reassures him, causing him to relax.

So make a point of moving around your horse with rhythm and purpose. Don't be timid and slow because a horse picks up on any hesitation. The more still you are and the less you move, the more quickly a horse loses confidence in you as a leader. But the more you move around your horse, the more relaxed he becomes because he confidently looks to you as his leader.

Don't make things such that your horse must become the leader. Your horse will take the offensive if you don't.

"You can avoid a lot of problems down the road by starting out with the right horse."

3

GETTING PERSONAL

You can't begin to understand a horse, let alone build a relationship with one, until you admit that every horse is a unique individual. Because of that, you can't approach each horse in the same way. Your techniques with different horses might be similar, but the application varies, depending on the horse, and this is something a good horseman learns through experience.

For instance, I might have a horse that fights the bit and doesn't want to become soft through his poll. Instead of working on that horse's head, I focus on gaining control and softness with my legs, by getting the horse to bend his body. When I

"Pepto" brings unique personality traits and a willing disposition to his job as a clinician's "demo" horse.

31

again ask him to break at the poll, he's much more likely to do so after he's soft and yielding through his body.

Unique Individuals

Every horse has a unique personality even though there can be similarities among horses, as well as among certain breeds and bloodlines. Some horses are softer personalities, while others are strong characters.

"Your horse needs you to be a leader more than he needs you to be his friend."

The better you know your horse, the more you understand how to work successfully with him. As you work with more horses, you discover that some have more consistent personalities, in that they're the same whether you're on the ground or in the saddle. Other horses are very easygoing until you actually ask them to perform.

Personally, I don't pay much attention to the differences between mares and geldings; I think horsemanship is more about recognizing individual personalities than about males or females. I love to ride good mares; they have a lot of heart. On the other hand, not all stallions make good performance or using horses, and some offspring are much better than the stallions ever were.

But I have found that each horse is born with a distinctive trait that might be from his sire or his dam, or even reach back a generation. Even with young foals, I can see the personality differences when they're with their dams or playing with other foals, and whether they're brave and courageous or timid and cautious.

You can tell a lot about a horse by watching his eye; the strength of his personality shows in his eyes. Intelligence, kindness, willingness, fear or panic—all are revealed through the horse's eye. You can tell when a horse feels settled by studying his eye.

When a horse gets the consistency he craves, he develops into a reliable performer.

It takes only a focused look to move the horse's hip because he's learned from routine cueing and follow-through during previous training sessions.

Avoid Personality Conflicts

I've found that a surprising number of horse owners, especially first-time owners, don't really consider personality when choosing a horse. A person often is drawn to a horse for the wrong reasons. Color and beauty are important, but they should never be the deciding factors when buying a horse. Just as with seeking a human partner, personality and suitability should be primary concerns when looking for a horse.

That gorgeous buckskin colt you have your heart set on, or that fiery black mare with the spark in her eye, might not be the right horse for you if your personalities don't mesh. In addition, your ability and knowledge must match the horse's personality and experience in order to have a good partnership. A sensitive horse with a high energy level won't require as much assertiveness when you correct and work with him. Likewise, a lazier horse with less forward motion requires more energy and assertiveness on your part.

The bottom line: You must be brutally honest about your abilities when shopping for a horse. The more experience and knowledge you gain, the more effective you can be in dealing with a wide range of horses. But if you're starting out or are an intermediate rider, it's important to have a horse whose personality can enhance, not deter, your learning. Once you've built your confidence, feel and timing with that horse, you can apply the same techniques to more challenging horses with greater and greater success.

> ## "So much of being a success with horses is about being consistent."

You can avoid a lot of problems down the road by starting with the right horse. If you are new or fairly new to riding, seek professional advice and find a horse that already has a proven track record of looking after his rider. He might not be the color of your dream horse, and he might have a few miles on him, and, in fact, he should. But the key is finding a first horse that is a joy to ride so

It's easy enough for a rider, microphone in hand, to communicate with other people, but only consistent use of body language can ensure that she and her horse stay in sync.

you can build your confidence, apply your techniques and improve your skills.

Whatever you do, don't make the mistake of pairing a young, green horse with an inexperienced or nervous rider. A novice rider needs a solid, seasoned and mature horse as teacher and guide.

"The motivation and confidence we gain in working with horses shows up in everything we do in life."

You need to gain confidence and skill before you can successfully handle a young horse because he is much more sensitive and unpredictable than an older, well-trained horse. Once you've ridden many horses and can reschool an older horse, polishing all the techniques on him that you would apply to a

young colt, that's when you're ready to start a green horse.

Horses are like clothes. Like it or not, you do outgrow some horses. This doesn't mean you have to sell them, but realize that you might need another horse with more ability. Once you've accomplished all you can with a horse, you can't continue to improve if you don't step up to another horse that offers different challenges and requires you to become a better horseman or horsewoman.

Common Mistakes

Even when you find a good match in a horse whose personality suits yours, you still can make serious mistakes when working with that horse. There's an old saying, "A one-eyed man is king in the land of the blind," and we're all guilty at some point of thinking we know more than we actually do.

At expos and clinics, I see many common errors that horse owners routinely make. More often than not, they don't do these things intentionally, but need to polish their skills, or simply don't understand their horses. Let's look at a few of those mistakes.

Mistake 1: People become angry, impatient or passive with their horses.

Many years ago, when I first started helping people with their horses, I saw a trend of people becoming too aggressive. What they did wasn't working, so they became angry and took out their anger on their horses. Whenever I see someone who's rough on a horse, I see someone who's come to the end of his knowledge. If I start to get frustrated when I work a horse, I realize that I'm coming to the end of my knowledge, and this motivates me to learn more instead of becoming angry.

Keeping your cool doesn't mean you shouldn't be firm with a horse; you must always be effective. But you can't be effective if you lose your cool and let anger take over the situation.

Don't take it personally when a horse does something wrong. Don't hold a grudge; don't try to "get even" with him. If your horse does something dangerous, you need to be assertive, firm and effective. You must correct him; then let up on the pressure as soon as you get the response you need.

Today, most people I see at clinics are too passive and actually teach their horses to become dangerous. This goes back to the issue of being friends with a horse.

Your horse needs you to be a leader more than he needs you to be his friend. He won't respect you if you can't or won't lead. Treats and petting do not overcome or solve bad behavior.

Mistake 2: People fail to communicate clearly in ways the horse can understand.

Always keep in mind that any body language is crucial—both yours and your horse's. This is how the horse relates to you, and you're a step ahead if you remember this. Your horse instinctively understands the demeanor and expression of your body and face. How quickly or slowly you move, how you distribute your weight, leaning toward or away from your horse, and whether you move passively or purposefully are things that send direct messages to the horse.

I personally don't use much in the way of verbal cues around my horses. Instead, I rely on putting that expression into my body for the horse to read. I've found that the more I use my voice, the less I use my body, and that shouldn't be the case.

Know that you can communicate clearly with your horse without necessarily saying a word out loud.

Mistake 3: People "lie" to their horses.

So much of being a success with horses is about being consistent. If you are inconsistent and don't follow through when handling your horse, you literally "lie" to him. Some owners confuse their horses by not using the same cues each time. Others might cue correctly, but don't persist until the horse responds correctly. Both examples show inconsistency, and you must remember that your horse craves consistency.

If you want positive results, you can't be hit and miss by handling your horse inconsistently. Your horse is a product of the training skills you apply. Even a great horse won't respond well unless you know how to raise your energy level and ask him to perform accordingly.

A solid training program is built in a progression of steps, and even the simplest step becomes the foundation for an advanced maneuver.

The horse, through no fault of his own, hasn't learned how to find his natural head-set, but can learn when his rider progresses through the proper steps.

Many times an owner assumes that his horse understands what he is being asked to do and that his horse is being disobedient. The horse seeks weakness and takes advantage of it.

Remember: Horses understand if you're hesitant, timid or uncertain. This is why a horse bucks with one person, but not with another rider. That type of horse needs a dominant, assertive leader. If he can step into the saddle and become the leader by instigating activity—telling the horse what to do and how much to do it—the horse won't even think about acting up or bucking.

Mistake 4: People ask their horses for too much too soon.

Everything you do with your horse should be built in a progression of steps. In fact, building a horsemanship program is exactly like building a staircase. You can't expect to arrive at the top unless you climb all the steps to get there.

Clear communication between horse and handler leads to a respectful, working partnership.

Practically Speaking: The Comfort Zone

Most any broke horse that you work regularly can get into a comfort zone. He falls into a pattern of doing and accepting the same things. This horse can react unexpectedly if you put additional pressure on him and ask him to move out of his comfort zone.

You might ask him to back more quickly than usual, and he might respond by throwing his head. Or you might cue him to step up the pace at the canter, and he kicks out or swishes his tail.

Riders at my clinics often say, "My horse never does this at home."

But I explain that they've never asked their horses for this much before.

If you ride in an arena most of the time, when you take your horse for a trail ride, he reacts differently—even when you give him the same cues and ask for the same responses you do at home. This is because the new environment puts additional pressure on your horse and reveals his insecurities or deficiencies, and yours as a rider, which you wouldn't see in the arena.

This doesn't mean you can't ask your horse for more. You can and should "raise the bar" and ask more of your horse. But – and here's the secret: Don't ask for more until you've progressed step-by-step through each skill level where you currently are working and until he satisfactorily completes each task. You don't tackle calculus until you've mastered algebra.

Even when a horse has the necessary foundation because you've taken the necessary time, he still needs to gain confidence and skill at any task. But if you've done your homework, he should catch on fairly quickly.

Asking your horse to perform a task or maneuver he isn't prepared to do, or doesn't understand because he doesn't have the foundation, is asking only for failure. You want to set up your horse to succeed, not fail. You can help set him up for success by building skills step-by-step and by not moving on until you've accomplished each lesson along the way. If every horse owner worked gradually to perfect the skills it takes to move to the next level of horsemanship, there would be much less injury and much more enjoyment with horses.

Asking too much too soon also applies to you as a horseman or horsewoman. Riding is not only about training the horse, but also about preparing and training yourself. Once you do that, it's easy to train your horse because he can accept the techniques you apply. But you need to learn – and continue learning – in order to improve your relationship with your horse.

I always say that anyone who is successful with horses learns directly from the horses. I think people often are impatient and don't fully understand the time and effort that it takes to become really good with horses.

You must adopt the mindset that you're on a mission to work on your inadequacies, to perfect your feel, timing and awareness, and to be more sensitive to what the horse tells you—all the things it takes to effectively communicate with that animal. If you have a systematic training program, this encourages you and builds your confidence. Then you get into a groove, and the desire to better yourself becomes addictive. As you improve, every horse you work with should become better and better.

I always can learn more and do better. This is what motivates me; I'm always looking for ways to improve my horsemanship skills.

To improve your riding, find someone skilled with horses, whose horsemanship demonstrates his or her knowledge and ability, and follow that person's example. If you emulate someone average, you never will be anything but average; if you emulate someone excellent, you become excellent.

The motivation and confidence we gain in working with horses shows up in everything we do in life. The horse is just a vehicle to help us get there. I think God put horses here on earth for us to enjoy and also to learn a lot of life's lessons.

"To me, natural horsemanship means understanding how the horse's mind works and using this knowledge to work with—not against—his natural instincts."

4

THE PSYCHOLOGY OF HORSEMANSHIP

Ever since man figured out he could climb on a horse's back and ride, we have been fascinated with this amazing animal.

Through the centuries, we've used horses to fight wars, conquer enemies, create empires, explore new territories, build countries, cultivate crops, hunt food, defend borders, deliver goods and mail, move cattle and clear land. We've also used the horse for entertainment and for pleasure, and for many owners this has become the horse's dominant purpose.

Intelligent horsemanship involves understanding the horse well enough to head off problems before they occur, rather than trying to fix problems afterward.

Ironically, there are more horses in North America today than at any time in history, even though the majority of people no longer use horses for work. The good news for the horse is that advances in technology and veterinary medicine, and a renewed interest in horsemanship knowledge, make it possible for these animals to live healthier, happier lives than ever before.

In today's horsemanship climate, "natural" is popular. Natural horsemanship can mean different things, depending on whom you ask. To me, natural horsemanship means understanding how the horse's mind works and using this knowledge to work with—not against—his natural instincts. It also means not using props, gimmicks and special equipment to train the horse.

The key is to get into the horse's mind and understand what he thinks before his feet start moving and he gets into trouble. By understanding what is going on inside his head, you can head off problems before they occur. You can call it being a "natural horse-

man," or you can simply think of it as intelligent horsemanship.

Avoid Extremes

I think it was Mae West who said, "Too much of a good thing is wonderful." In many ways she has a point, but when it comes to horsemanship, we have to be careful of going to extremes.

I see great examples of this all the time in my clinics and horsemanship courses. There are two extremes in how many people handle horses: They're either too aggressive or too passive. We touched on this in the last chapter, but I think it's important to devote some more time to these topics since they are surprisingly common.

Too Aggressive

It doesn't take long to discover if someone has a tendency to be aggressive with his horse. Horses have a way of bringing out our

A clinician on tour often takes the role of equine psychologist to work effectively and in a timely manner with a variety of horses.

This once-resistant horse at a tour stop began to follow my direction when he accepted my leadership.

worst emotional qualities pretty darned fast. I usually can spot someone who has issues with anger and aggression in a matter of minutes, just by watching him work with his horse.

Typically, there is no smoothness in the way an aggressive person handles a horse. His actions and body language lack rhythm and fluidity; he is quick to react and show his temper. He is abrupt with his cues and overly dominant. He doesn't like to wait and give the horse time to think through things. As a result, the horse becomes more "slave" than partner in the relationship. Watch the horse, and he is not a happy animal. He might perform because he "has" to, but he generally shows signs of fear, confusion and/or resentment.

In my opinion, a tendency toward aggression traces directly back to early upbringing and childhood. I had to learn to overcome the tendency to get angry because I knew it would keep me from becoming the horseman I wanted to be. Instead of blaming the horse for doing something "wrong," I had to acknowledge the emotion rising within me. I had to become more balanced in my personality, more consistent, and this translated to my human interactions, too.

Any time you lose your temper, you lose control. As I've said before, frustration is a sign that you lack preparation and knowledge. To be successful with horses, you must be able to think and reason; you can't just attack the situation with force. This does not mean you can't be firm with a horse, but force and firmness are different things, just as assertiveness differs from aggression. Every good horseperson has to be firm with a horse at times. It's how you correct and teach your horse that is important. You can be firm, but you must be conscious of what you're doing and consistent in your approach. It's impossible to remain consistent when you're angry. When that adrenaline sets in—with horse or human—neither can think clearly.

My entire life is built around the relationship I have with the horse. I always want my horse to know he can depend on me to be reliable and consistent. I strive to be as consistent as possible with my horse, whether he's giving me a hard time or not.

Taking that approach doesn't mean you don't have emotions, but you don't want to get too "high" or too "low" emotionally around the horse because you want your body language to remain consistent. You want to keep the tension out of your body because doing so makes it much easier for your horse to understand what you ask of him. If you have to take a break and walk away for a few minutes, then, by all means, do.

Just as there are people who rub you the wrong way for no apparent reason, you're

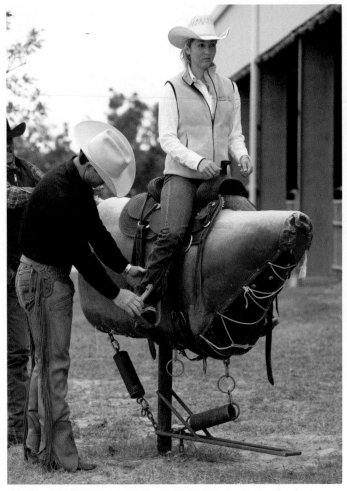

The barrel machine enables a rider to better master the feel, timing and balance needed to become an offensive, proactive rider in control.

bound to come across a horse or two that always seems to challenge you. This goes back to the personalities that don't mesh. But make no mistake, even when you have a horse whose personality suits you fine, there still are times when you become frustrated with him. How you respond – not react— shows the level of your emotional control and your horsemanship skill.

A horse's survival instinct leads him to try to get the better of you. Like it or not, a horse treats you just like he treats another horse. In a group situation, horses always try to dominate each other. The milder-mannered, less dominant horses try to flee and escape the situation. If you ride enough horses, you also meet some stubborn individuals, who try to push your buttons. Just like a strong-willed child, that type of horse pushes until you set boundaries and give clear direction.

Whenever the human doesn't give clear direction and/or leadership, the horse looks to his own leadership and forms his own program going in his own direction. He always seeks the easiest way. This is not a flaw; it's just the horse's nature.

Too Passive

At the other end of the spectrum from the overly aggressive horse owner is someone who lets the horse dominate. That person offers no leadership to the horse and, as a result, the horse ends up in control, which is neither wise nor safe.

So if your horse calls all the shots, you're in trouble.

I believe people who are too passive often don't truly understand horses. They don't realize that a horse, just like a person, can take advantage of a situation.

When you are too passive, you offer "suggestions" to the horse, not clear direction. And since, as you know, a horse likes to do what is easiest, more often than not, he doesn't take your suggestion seriously. There's a lot of miscommunication because the passive rider doesn't tend to follow through on his requests consistently, and he or she usually is not assertive with actions and cues. Horses are quick to pick up on such hesitancy and uncertainty.

Through the years, I've met plenty of people who are very accomplished and confident in their professional and business lives, but lose that confidence as soon as they get around horses. The people's actions and body language start to change, and their horses immediately sense this loss of confidence. In this situation, I encourage the people to recall how they feel when they're confidently in charge in the other areas of their lives, and have them picture themselves being this way around the horse.

"Knowledge and ability can replace fear and anxiety."

Interestingly enough, today I see more passive, timid horsemen and -women than aggressive ones. I think this is basically due to lack of knowledge, but fear also plays a role. Even if an observer doesn't notice, when you have fearful or nervous energy, it goes right into your horse.

Conquer Fear

Because of a huge demand and many requests, I began holding courses at my ranch specifically for people dealing with fear. More often than not, they aren't beginning riders. Many are horse owners who have ridden for years, but have had bad spills or wrecks with horses, which changed each person's entire perspective. In some cases, it was a freak accident; in others, a poor decision on the human's part led to the incident. Sometimes the rider was simply in a bad situation, or he might have been riding a horse he wasn't prepared to ride. Whatever the reason, fear has colored these riders' lives with horses, and those people live with that fear every day.

I look at these courses more as psychology lessons, rather than horsemanship lessons, because they are strategically designed to build the rider's confidence. I put these individuals in positions where they succeed by creating situations in which they can accomplish the task at hand. This builds their confidence, and then they go to the next task. We actually work more with the people, rather than the horses, by increasing the people's

knowledge and skill levels, which in turn raises their confidence.

Fear and anxiety can be overwhelming, paralyzing emotions. The thing many people don't understand: You can't just tell yourself, "I'm not going to be afraid. I'm not going to be nervous."

> *"Once we understand the techniques and know how to apply those techniques, the horses will let us know when we have it right."*

When you do that, you actually focus on those negative emotions. Instead, you have to develop a substitute; you must replace those emotions with something else, or they continue to dominate. That's why I use the slogan, "Building Confidence through Knowledge." When I can show someone how to increase his skill, when I help him learn techniques that give him control, then his focus switches

A horse is a great teacher, and an honest one that lets us know the areas where we need to work.

to something positive. Knowledge and ability can replace fear and anxiety.

Most riders taking my courses on overcoming fear with knowledge bring their own horses, sometimes the very same horses with which the people had the wrecks or bad situations. In some cases the horse is dangerous, so I work to get the horse safe enough for the person to handle and ride. If it's actually a bad match between horse and rider, I have to be honest and tell someone this isn't the horse he needs at this point in his life.

During the course, we always start work on the ground first, and these people learn how to polish their feel and timing and how to

"If your horse is resistant in his attitude and response, he's telling you that your approach needs polish and refinement."

change their body language to be more assertive, so their horses clearly understand what the people are asking. Before they get in the saddle, I put the riders on a barrel machine so they really learn to find their balance and correct seat positions. I want them to become offensive riders.

You don't want to be on the defensive when you ride; this is how accidents happen. If you are an offensive rider, you're in control. Most people sit on a horse and wait for something to happen. By the time it does and they react, it's too late.

Being an offensive rider means that you have a plan, and you put the horse to work. You get his feet to move; you change his mind if he has a negative reaction, such as bucking, shying, or rearing. The offensive rider doesn't just sit in the saddle; he thinks all the time. He takes charge and is in control of his horse. When his horse feels that his rider is in control, it actually calms the horse because he always looks for direction.

If you can't give this direction to a horse, especially one who is anxious or green, he is going to act on his own, and that usually isn't positive. That's why you must have a

program, a system, when you work with horses. When you ask a horse to do a task and ask him with assertive, confident energy, your horse starts to relax and accepts your leadership.

Changing Ourselves

Whether we like to admit it or not, we all have things we need to change and grow in order to become better horsemen and -women. One of the greatest things about the horse is that he tells us so much about ourselves. If we are honest and listen, he lets us know the areas where we need to work.

"I had no idea what I didn't know!" is the most common feedback I hear from people who take courses at the ranch. This comes from all kinds of people: white collar, blue collar, hobby riders and those who make their livings with horses.

Sometimes we flat-out need an attitude adjustment. But in many cases, we simply need more knowledge, we need to refine our skills, and we need to be better prepared to work with horses. Once we understand the techniques and know how to apply those techniques, the horses let us know when we have things right. Many times we aren't clear in our cues and body language. We send confusing messages to our horses. When we get inconsistent responses from our horses, this might well be the case.

Are you being too assertive, too rough? If your horse is resistant in his attitude and response, he's telling you that your approach needs polish and refinement.

Watch your horse's reactions. Sometimes a horse is simply ignorant and doesn't know what you want. This usually is the case when you start a young, green horse. He's innocent and doesn't yet have a foundation for building skills. But with older horses and those that have been handled, you see a variety of responses, ranging from the horse being relaxed and content to being sour, confused, angry and frightened.

Use every opportunity with your horse to ask, "What is he saying about me?" As with a person, a horse sometimes can be in a lazy or uncooperative mood, but most of the time, his response relates directly to your approach. A horse is honest and doesn't worry about being politically correct. He tells it like it is. Your horse can be a great teacher if you pay attention.

Real People... Real Solutions

LAURA GARABEDIAN

"Chris doesn't just boost you up; he gives you a lot of strategies." Maria Glinski, DVM

Having ridden for years and been active in the demanding sport of eventing, Maria Glinski, DVM, considered herself a confident horsewoman. A small-animal practitioner in Aiken, S.C., Maria also lectures and teaches other veterinarians.

A breeder of Dutch Warmbloods, Maria was riding one of her young horses in the round pen when something startled him, and he began bucking. Maria came off, hitting the side of the round pen and injuring her arm and hand, which resulted in nerve damage and a long physical recovery.

She turned out her two Warmbloods for the year and, after recovering from her injury, continued to ride her older horse without incident. Not until the following year, when she got back on the younger Warmblood again, did she realize she had a problem.

"I'm a self-confident person with my own veterinary practice, so when I started to feel this fear, it surprised me because I feel very confident in other areas of my life," said Maria, who is in her 50s. "I had a professional trainer work with the horse. He's an incredibly sweet horse, but very reactive, and every time he'd make a sudden movement, I replayed the accident over again. I wanted to improve my riding and get over this, but when I started back with him and my other young horse, it all came right back.

"I found out about Chris because I went to Road to the Horse in March 2007. When I got my tickets to Road to the Horse, I went to the Web sites of all the participants, and I noticed that Chris gives a course on building rider confidence. I saw him ride (and win) at Road to the Horse and booked my space in his course the very next day.

"The course was one of the most powerful weeks of my life. Chris has a remarkable way of training people in increments the same way he trains horses. He's very intuitive and sees where your boundaries are and what your fears are. He takes you to the edge and just beyond, but not so you feel like you're falling off a cliff.

"I've been teaching other veterinarians for the last 20 years and because I'm a teacher myself, I realize how important it is to teach incrementally and not to overwhelm the student. Chris is a natural-born teacher and leader. He's very firm, very tough, and he makes you want to do well.

"There were about 20 of us in the course and every single person had different issues.

"Chris said over and over again, 'No matter what your problem is, no matter what your issue is, we can solve it.'

"Chris helps expose issues you might not even know you have. My fear went a lot deeper than I ever imagined. It was ugly at first, but I had to face it to get through to the other side. He showed me that I was actually creating a bucking issue with my horse because my horse realized I wasn't serious when I asked him to canter. He knew if he just gave a little buck at the canter I wouldn't ask him to go on. Chris had his assistant get on my horse, and this was really powerful for me because she was able to get him to canter, ride through the bucking and make him go on. I saw how strong and assertive she had to be, and this gave me a visual image of what I had to do. It also gave me more confidence. At some of the clinics I've been to, the instructors won't get on your horse, but Chris is willing to do whatever it takes to help you.

"This course made me look at other areas of my life, not just my riding. I started digging deeper into patterns in my life and asking myself, 'Where am I not being clear and assertive?'

"Our horses are mirrors of ourselves, the way they move or don't move and the way they act out. Now I am so much better at communicating with my horse. Chris doesn't just boost you up, he give you a lot of strategies. Now I have the skills and tools I need to communicate clearly with my horse.

"I would definitely classify Chris as a natural horsemanship trainer because he's so in tune with the horse and knows how to communicate with him on his level. What makes Chris different is that his techniques are very practical, and he really believes that the horse is a working animal that loves to have a job. I realized my horse is happier when he has a job and knows what expect.

"One of the highlights was at the end of the week when I was driving cattle on my 5-year-old Dutch Warmblood, Valiant. It was great! He was having fun, and I could feel his confidence. Even though the course is about rider confidence, my horse's confidence also increased. There is no way at the beginning of the week that he could have been driving cattle."

Maria has booked space to return to Chris' ranch and take Horsemanship I, riding the horse on which she had her accident, so she can create a solid foundation with him, and leave the fear behind permanently.

**"To me, natural horsemanship
is using the least
equipment necessary to
get effective results."**

5

EQUIPMENT 101

W hen you build a house, you need the right tools to get the job done; you won't get much accomplished if all you have is a hammer. Whether you're a carpenter, a mechanic, an artist or a horseman, without the tools of your trade, you're stuck. You can have the best theories and skills in the world, but without the right equipment you won't get very far.

Through the years, I've used plenty of different tack and equipment, and have come up with some specific things I like to use simply because I think they work the best for me. I am never

Only when the rider knows how to use his leg effectively in all three leg positions can he even consider using spurs.

When working afoot, a knotted rope halter and an attached 13-foot lead are invaluable tools for directing and driving a horse.

going to tell you that you can't get results if you don't use the same equipment, but I will share with you what I prefer to use and why. Safety is a very important reason behind some of the equipment I use. I'm also big on practicality; if something can make me a more effective horseman, then I'm all for it.

"The lead rope serves as both a directional tool and a correctional tool, depending on whether you use the front or the tail end of the rope."

I firmly believe that technique and ability are far more important than relying on more equipment. To me, natural horsemanship is using the least equipment necessary to get effective results. Yes, I need certain tools to work with my horse, but the way I look at it: The more equipment I have to use, the more

I get away from improving my natural horse-manship. Tie-downs and mechanical devices shouldn't take the place of solid horsemanship.

This chapter can't cover every piece of tack that might be needed, but it does focus on the basics I use every day and how to use the tack effectively.

Halter and Lead Rope

Some of the most important tools ever used when working with a horse are the halter and lead rope. There are a number of different halters and halter-lead rope combinations available. I have designed and use a one-piece knotted rope halter with an attached 13-foot lead rope. The lead rope is slightly weighted and has a leather popper on the end, which can make noise, but doesn't sting the horse at all. The popper also adds balance to the rope.

There are a number of reasons I prefer this arrangement, with safety and control being priorities. Unlike a conventional nylon or leather halter, the rope halter has no buckles or metal rings to bend or break. Because the halter and lead rope are combined, I never have to worry about hardware breaking when my horse is tied or when I work with him.

I dislike the traditional lead rope with snap hook because I've seen a lot of accidents due to snaps breaking under pressure. Not only can that end up with a loose horse in a bad situation, but also with people being permanently injured by a breaking snap hitting them in the head.

If a tied horse learns just once that he can pull back and get loose because the halter and/or lead rope breaks, he always will try to pull until he is consistently tied with a halter and lead that hold.

Your halter and lead are invaluable when it comes to groundwork. The lead rope serves as both a directional tool and a correctional tool, depending on whether you use the front or the tail end of the rope. Direction is always given with the front part of the rope closest to the horse's head, while correction and drive come from the tail end. You also can use your lead rope to reinforce a cue given where your leg would be on the horse if you were mounted.

In upcoming chapters, whenever I refer to your "direction" hand, remember that is always the hand closest to your horse's head. It might be your right or left hand,

Practically Speaking: The Pecking Order

In a group of horses, the lower a horse is in the pecking order, the more he uses his feet. He's always moving to get out of the way of more dominant horses. Keep this in mind because, from the horse's perspective, the more he can make you move your feet, the less of a leader you are.

The main reason I use a 13-foot lead rope: It allows me to accomplish a lot with a horse without moving my feet much at all. When the horse challenges me—and he will—I have more to work with by using a longer rope. The horse ends up moving his feet more than I do, and this is something he clearly understands. It tells him who is in control.

depending on which side of the horse you are working. Your "driving" hand is always the hand closest to the tail end of the rope.

I know some horsemen use a stick to work horses afoot, but I use the rope instead because I always have the halter and lead rope on the horse when doing groundwork or leading him. I don't want to use an additional piece of equipment, a stick or a crop that I have to pick up because, once I set it down, the horse knows the difference.

Handling the Lead

Before you ever use your lead rope on your horse, you need to be familiar with handling the rope. In many situations you twirl your rope when teaching the horse.

Being able to twirl the lead effectively with either hand helps ensure that a horse works equally well in either direction.

You need to be comfortable with this technique so you can be smooth and fluid when handling your horse.

- Always keep your hand over the top of the lead rope.

- Twirl the rope in an overhand, not underhand motion. Twirling overhand gives you much more control of the lead rope.

- As you twirl your lead, let the rope feed through your hand to make the length of rope you twirl long or short.

- Use the last two fingers of your twirling hand to direct the rope and add or decrease your twirling speed.

- Practice these techniques until you're comfortable using the rope and twirl it equally well with both hands. Typically, you find that you handle the rope better on one side. However, your actions need to be balanced and smooth on both sides because doing so helps your horse become balanced on both sides.

Headstalls, Bits and Reins

For working a horse and general riding, I use a simple harness-leather headstall with a sliding browband and a throatlatch. I prefer this to a one-ear or split-ear headstall without a throatlatch because the horse can't rub or flip off the headstall by shaking his head.

I primarily use one of three bits that I've designed: a D-ring snaffle with a fixed mouthpiece and two styles of shanked curb bits. I use the D-ring snaffle most for training. After a horse is "finished" and when I compete with him, I change to a loose-jawed, shanked curb bit with a snaffle mouthpiece or a ported one.

However, when I start a young horse, I always make the first few rides using only the halter and the lead rope. Then I start riding the horse in the fixed D-ring snaffle. The fixed ring offers the horse more direction because the mouthpiece doesn't swivel. This bit's contoured mouthpiece also allows the bit to sit where it should in the horse's mouth, without pinching his bars. Because of the contours, this bit is especially effective for lateral work. The contoured

mouthpiece also is inlaid with copper to increase salivation, which helps the horse's mouth stay moist.

When using a regular snaffle without a fixed mouthpiece, it's important to always use a chinstrap, or bit hobble. The strap attaches to the snaffle rings, in front of the reins. The strap keeps the snaffle in place and prevents it from pulling through the horse's mouth. However, the strap shouldn't be tight; adjust it so that you easily can slide at least three fingers between the horse's chin and the strap.

Riders in my courses often ask when they should begin to use a shanked bit. I tell them they can make the change after they can accomplish everything they want to do with the horse in a snaffle bit. Some people mistakenly think that the more severe or heavier the bit put into a horse's mouth, the more the rider can accomplish with the horse. The truth: It's hands, knowledge and technique—not bits—that get results. If you can't get results with a snaffle, you only have more trouble when you step up to a more severe bit.

When working colts and young horses, I like to use a single loop rein, also called a sport rein, made of round, poly-cotton blend rope. I use a headstall and the rein with a 10-foot long mecate. Having a mecate is like having a lead rope built into my headgear; the mecate allows me to do groundwork and

The fixed D-rings on this contoured snaffle bit provide solid direction for the horse.

Having a mecate on the snaffle-bit headstall is much like having a lead rope built into the headgear.

When it's time to switch from a snaffle to a curb bit, this loose-jawed, shanked bit with a broken snaffle mouthpiece is a popular option.

Split leather reins can be attached to the fixed-ring snaffle, typically after a horse has progressed beyond the basics.

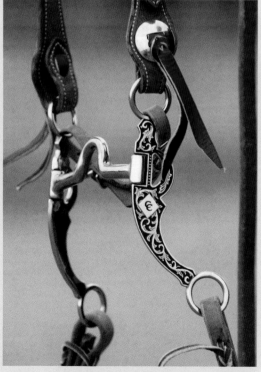

Another option when switching from a snaffle to curb bit is this loose-jawed, shanked bit with a ported mouthpiece.

even to tie my horse without putting pressure on his mouth. As a horse gets further along in his training, I use split leather reins, but for training I really like using the round rope sport rein with mecate.

Saddles and Pads

I might be a cowboy, but I'm very open-minded about different riding styles because of my background. Growing up in Pony Club in Australia, I rode a lot in an English saddle, as well as in Australian saddles.

I own a number of different Western saddles and have designed a custom all-around saddle made to my specifications by a saddlemaker here in Texas. I use that saddle for training, ranch work, roping, cutting and trail riding.

Whenever possible, I recommend buying a handmade saddle over a factory-made one. With care, a quality handmade saddle can last a good 30 years. If you have a factory-made saddle that fits your horse, I'm not going to say you have to spend more money to buy a handmade one.

My saddles are made with a little thinner leather than most, which makes the saddle lighter but, more important, puts me closer to my horse. I like a close-contact, centered, smooth leather seat without a lot of buildup. This allows me sit as closely as possible to my

horse's back for better communication. I actually have the saddlemaker cut away a portion of the skirt leather under my fenders, so only the thin fender is between my leg and the horse's side, which increases my leg contact.

I like all natural fleece under a saddle, instead of synthetic, because I think natural fleece offers better breatheability. I have back girths on all my saddles since the back girth helps the saddle remain stable on the horse's back. I prefer wooden, flat-bottomed stirrups, rather than metal or oxbow-style stirrups, but this is just my personal preference.

Wool felt pads cost more than synthetic pads, but I think that wool is the best type of saddle pad. Wool is a natural fiber and dissipates pressure on the horse's back. A pad with wear leathers lasts much longer than one without. When the same pad is used regularly on the same horse, the pad, in time, actually conforms to that horse's back.

I use both neoprene and leather girths with wool fleece lining, and like both styles. I insist on using leather latigos, although I know a lot of people like nylon. I don't use nylon because nylon doesn't give when a horse breathes, and anyone can seriously overtighten a nylon latigo. Latigo leather is designed to stretch. Be sure to check your latigos regularly. There shouldn't be any cracks or slight tears in the leather; for

The pad or blanket should be centered on the horse's back, as well as underneath the saddle.

A natural wool pad helps dissipate pressure on a horse's back.

In time and with regular use, a wool felt pad eventually conforms to the horse's back.

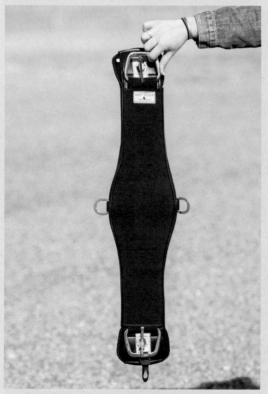

A neoprene girth is easy to clean and comfortable for most horses.

This girth is lined with natural wool fleece for comfort.

A misplaced saddle is uncomfortable for the horse and increases the rider's difficulty in maintaining accurate balance and timing.

Even when a saddle fits a horse well, the saddle must be correctly positioned for maximum benefit.

Practically Speaking: Improper Saddle Fit

Be sure your saddle fits your horse. Improper saddle fit can cause a horse to:

- object to being saddled.
- become sore-backed and sensitive.
- switch his tail.
- pin his ears.
- toss his head.
- be reluctant to relax.
- be reluctant or refuse to change leads.
- lack extension, or have a shortened stride.
- move choppily.
- be unable to use hindquarters properly.
- experience muscle atrophy.
- experience lameness problems.

safety's sake you need to replace them before they get too worn.

One problem I do see: Riders seldom check their equipment. Many wrecks could be avoided if riders checked their equipment each time they saddled their horses. Look over your tack every time you ride.

Saddle Fit and Placement

The important thing—whether a saddle is handmade or factory-made—is that it fits the horse properly. Too many horse owners ride saddles that actually cause their horses physical pain and problems. But because the saddles are comfortable to the riders, each person thinks his saddle fits his horse.

You might get away with using a saddle that doesn't fit correctly for a while, but in time a poor fit leads to problems, and your horse's physical performance will be compromised. Check for any dry spots on your horse's back when you unsaddle. The horse's back should be uniformly sweaty under the saddle. If your saddle doesn't fit correctly, too much pressure is concentrated in specific areas, and when used consistently, with time the saddle actually damages nerves, resulting in dry spots, and destroys pigment in those areas. That often is the reason horses have white saddle marks on their backs.

Your saddle is built on a tree, which is just like a skeleton. If the tree bars don't properly fit your horse's back, the saddle won't fit, no matter how pretty it is on top. If you have any doubts about your saddle fitting your particular horse, consult a saddlemaker or saddle fitter.

One more comment on saddle fit: Don't rely on a pad to "fix" a saddle that doesn't fit. If your boots don't fit, you can't make them right by changing your socks. The same principle applies to saddles and pads.

Even if your saddle fits, you still must put it in the correct place on your horse's back.

Many people put their saddles too forward. They look at the D-ring placement on the saddle, where the girth attaches, and use that as a guide, so that the girth is right behind the horse's elbow. By doing that, the saddle often is too far forward, and the tree actually rests on top of the horse's scapula, or shoulder blade. This can sore a horse, limit his front-end movement, shorten his stride and make him stiff. The saddle should be placed so that it fits just behind the scapula.

When you saddle, always reach under the saddle gullet and pull loose any mane hairs under the pad. Then lift the front of the pad into the gullet so you create a "tunnel" that allows air to flow under the saddle. Also make sure your pad is placed evenly under the saddle; there should be at least an inch of pad in front of the saddle skirt. When saddling, wrap your latigo around the dee at least twice. If you have a back cinch, fasten it last and always undo it first.

> "If a rider thinks he or she absolutely has to have spurs to get the horse to do something, then he or she definitely doesn't need to ride with spurs."

The surest way to make your horse "cinchy" is to tighten your girth snugly all at once when you first saddle him. I always adjust my girth at least three times, gradually tightening it before I step into the saddle. I initially lead the horse a short distance, maybe do a few minutes of groundwork, and then adjust it again.

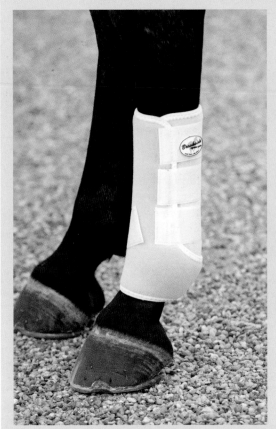

Leg gear helps protect a young horse that might be a bit clumsy when he first learns his job.

Polo wraps help support the suspensory ligaments on high-performance horses.

Although it might be convenient to lay your saddle pad on top of your saddle in the tack room, don't get in this habit. Hang your pad where it can dry without the salt from the horse's sweat contacting the leather, since this deteriorates the stitching and saddle leather in time.

Just a word about breast collars. Many people incorrectly use a breast collar to try to make a saddle fit a horse. Often a person adjusts a breast collar too tightly on his horse's shoulders, which means the saddle can't move down into the scapula area, where the saddle's supposed to sit. A too-tight breast collar results in restricting your horse's movement, and a too-loose breast collar can rub the points of his shoulders.

I use a breast collar, but use it loosely for roping or when I'm dragging something or traveling uphill. Although I do have regular breast collars, the pulling collar is what I really prefer because it stays up and in the V of my horse's neck. A pulling collar doesn't come straight across my horse's front end and inhibit his shoulder movement.

Spurs

Many riders who come to a ranch course want to ride with spurs. A common question is, "How do I know when I should use spurs?"

My thought: If a rider thinks he or she absolutely has to have spurs to get the horse to do something, then he or she definitely doesn't need to ride with spurs. A horse moves off a competent rider's legs before that person begins riding with spurs.

Learning how to use spurs properly is a part of becoming a knowledgeable horseman or -woman. But if you don't know how to use spurs correctly, they also can desensitize the horse, and even be a danger. Spurs can be a great addition to your horsemanship, but only when you are knowledgeable enough to use them. I discuss the use of spurs in Chapter 7 when I cover seat and leg positions.

Protective Leg Gear

I definitely advocate using protective leg wear on horses, but I use it only at the right times and for the right reasons. If used incor-

Practically Speaking: Leather or Synthetics?

I know a lot of riders who use tack made of nylon or synthetic materials. I'm sure there are plenty of reasons why someone would want a headstall or saddle made of something other than leather, but I can't think of one.

There are reasons why good tack always has been made of leather. Yes, leather requires regular care to stay in good condition, and leather usually costs more than synthetics. But leather tack lasts a long time with proper care, and leather stretches. It also "breathes" and feels better against a horse's skin, or human skin for that matter.

You can cut costs in some areas in horse ownership without a problem, but I can't recommend buying nylon or plastic tack.

---

rectly, leg protection can do a horse more harm than good.

I use polo wraps on my high-performance horses because the wraps help support their suspensory ligaments. I use protective boots on a young horse if he's a little clumsy when I start working and riding him.

But I also believe anyone can protect a horse too much by using protection too early in the horse's life. A horse needs to learn how to place his feet safely, and when he bumps himself early on, he learns to be more careful. Too much padding can be a detriment to that.

I don't agree with using leg protection on trail rides for several reasons. Debris and sand can get caught between the leg and a wrap or boot, and the friction can irritate the horse's leg and cause problems. Wraps and boots also can generate a lot of heat on the horse's legs, which I don't want.

When you use wraps and boots, you also must use them correctly. If the leg gear is put on the horse too tightly or positioned wrong, too low or crooked, the wraps or boots can cause the horse suspensory problems and even bow a tendon.

When it comes to leg wear for horses, there are many products available. Be sure you know how and when to use that gear so that it actually protects your horse, instead of causing damage.

"If you learn to be effective with groundwork, you get the horse's attention and accomplish your goals without having to spend a lot of time doing repetitious lessons afoot."

6

GROUNDWORK: WHERE IT ALL BEGINS

Everything you eventually do with your horse begins with groundwork. This is why I stress the importance of building a solid foundation on the ground before you ever get on the horse's back.

Groundwork is all about taking tension out of the horse's body. Groundwork is about achieving softness and suppleness, and gaining control and respect. My program allows you to be very effective with your groundwork so you can advance systematically with your horse. Groundwork is an important part of the overall program, but is only the foundation. If you learn

Take groundwork to the pasture to keep the basics from becoming boring, bland and repetitious for you and your horse.

to be effective with groundwork, you get the horse's attention and accomplish your goals without having to spend a lot of time doing repetitious lessons afoot.

Many people do so much groundwork that it actually takes away from their riding. Riding should be the priority; horses were made to be ridden. Once you establish the groundwork fundamentals, you don't have to keep going over and over these points. Yes, you must reassure and remind the horse as your horsemanship progresses, but you can make a horse sour and dull if you constantly drill him on the same things. You can always do more groundwork, if needed, but it's hard to go back and rebuild a program when you've done too much groundwork.

Ultimately, for me, the true test is in the saddle. Most tasks we do with horses are done while we're on their backs. Groundwork lays the foundation for this, but there are limits to what I can accomplish on the ground. The older a horse gets, the less groundwork I do.

Once your horse has mastered groundwork lessons, you need to move ahead and continue to advance your relationship from the saddle. Don't let fear and insecurity keep you on the ground.

"A round pen actually can limit forward motion and the horse's mobility, so don't rely on the round pen for security."

Tools and Pointers

For basic groundwork lessons, all you need is your halter and lead rope. Many people believe they must use a round pen with young horses, but I think this goes back to relying too much on equipment, rather than on technique and feel. Some trainers swear by a round pen, but I'm not one of those people. I would rather do groundwork in a large confined area, such as an arena or corral, instead of a round pen, although I do use a round pen for the initial stages of colt-starting.

Through the years, I've learned how to improve my techniques to better my horse and myself. I've found that I can accomplish a lot with a horse on the end of a lead rope—without having to run the horse around and around the pen, using all his energy.

Working a horse in a round pen too long can put boundaries on the horse's mind, and you don't want that. A round pen actually can limit forward motion and the horse's mobility, so don't rely on the round pen for security. There are only so many times a horse can go around in a circle in the same tracks again and again without losing interest in his work. There's no adventure there for the horse.

When I do use a round pen, I frequently "quarter" the horse, meaning that I make him change directions at a quarter-point of the pen, or a fourth of the way around the circle, rather than running him around and around the pen. Quartering lets me gain control of the horse quickly without exhausting him. Some horses run until they drop, and, believe me, an exhausted horse gasping for air is not going to learn. The horse must have air in order to concentrate; I don't want to wear him out so he's huffing and puffing.

Another reason I like doing groundwork in an area larger than a round pen is because I want to give the horse more room to make mistakes. This might sound contradictory, but some of our greatest lessons in life come from mistakes we've made and learned to work through to solutions.

Although many people want to prevent their horses from making mistakes, if you let your horse make a mistake, you then can correct and guide him in the right direction. If you always put your horse in a bubble and protect him from the mistakes, he always challenges you. This situation is similar to that of the rider who insists on always having hold of his horse's mouth; that hold actually makes the horse fight his rider.

Catch Your Horse

It's amazing how much time people waste trying to catch some horses. Rather than trying to "catch" my horses, I prefer to teach my horses to be caught. If you learn this method, you can use it no matter if your horse is in a stall, corral or large pasture.

Capturing a horse's attention while still some distance from him is the first step in teaching him to be caught.

Still at a distance, moving the horse's hindquarters to the right and left invites him to follow and controls his direction.

Turning and walking away from a horse draws him to his leader-handler and encourages him to follow.

Teaching a horse to drop his head on cue is a practical skill that makes haltering or bridling an easy routine.

Many people leave halters on loose horses "to make them easier to catch." It is potentially dangerous to leave a halter on a horse, since he can catch the halter on anything. The halter isn't needed when your horse knows how to be caught. Here's how to teach him.

- When you enter the pasture or corral where your horse is, step in front of him to capture his attention while you are some distance away from him. As soon as your horse's eyes and ears focus directly on you, stop and turn away. The key is to stop and release your pressure in coordination with the horse's response to you. The horse's confidence and desire to come to you build once he realizes you won't come into his space without his permission.

- Still standing at a distance from the horse, invite him toward you by moving his hind-quarters to the left and right. Do this by stepping in the direction opposite the way you want him to swing his rear end. For example, when you face the horse and step to your right, which is his left, he swivels to continue facing you,

which means he moves his hindquarters to his right. When you step to the left, as the horse faces you, he swivels his hind end to his left. Using this method, you can control your horse's movement even though you aren't close enough to touch him.

- Your horse's attention should be totally focused on you at this point, but notice that you haven't approached him or put on the halter. Now draw the horse to you by turning away from him again and walking to the gate.

- Slip on the halter only when the horse comes to you. Practice this method of teaching your horse to be caught, and you'll never have to go through the frustration of chasing him or trying to corner him to catch him.

Halter Your Horse

If you are unaccustomed to a rope halter, learn how to handle and tie one correctly so you can use it safely.

With the lead around the horse's neck, simply scoop his nose into the halter.

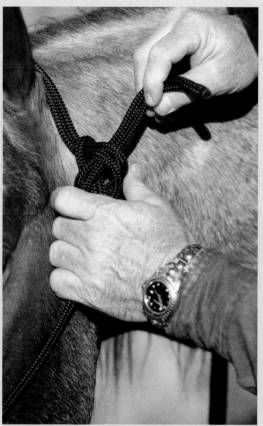

When tied correctly, the tail of the tied rope should point toward the horse's hindquarters.

- When haltering your horse, put the lead rope underneath and then over his neck. Hold the tail of the rope with your right hand and the halter with your left hand.

- Now grasp the halter crown rope in your right hand and the halter cheek loop in your left, and scoop your horse's nose into the halter as you slip it on him.

- Tie the halter crown rope in the cheek loop. When tying the sheepshank knot used to fasten a rope halter, the tail of the halter crown rope goes under and through the rope eye, and then over the eye loop and around to the right. Now bring the tail underneath the halter loop from right to left and feed the tail through the new loop you just made. Tighten the knot until the halter fits your horse appropriately. When the halter is tied, the tail of the tied rope should point to the rear, toward your horse's tail.

- When removing your halter, always keep the lead rope around the horse's neck for

added control as you untie and take off your halter.

- Never leave a halter on a loose horse. That is dangerous and unnecessary.

Lower the Head

Early on, I teach all my young horses to lower their heads on command. This teaches a horse respect, and is also practical because he becomes easier to handle and bridle. Gaining control of a horse's head also allows me to handle his ears.

- To teach your horse to lower his head, stand at his left side, and place your left hand on the bridge of the horse's nose and your right hand on his neck. Gently begin rocking his head from side to side using both hands.

- As soon as your horse starts to lower his head, release the pressure from both hands.

- Once your horse accepts this rocking motion by lowering his head, move your right hand from his neck to his poll and

With the left hand on the bridge of the horse's nose and the right at his poll, gently rock his head from side to side.

The moment the horse drops his head—no matter how slightly—release the pressure from both hands.

spread your fingers so that they cover the poll area. Your left hand remains on the bridge of his nose just for contact.

- Gently exert pressure on the poll with your right hand until your horse lowers his head. Keep in mind: You don't push down your horse's head. You just establish a hold, or a "brace," which is completely different from pushing.

- As soon as your horse lowers his head, release your right hand and rub his neck. Release the pressure from your left hand as well, although you can keep your thumb under the noseband when you do.

- For safety reasons, always stand next to the horse, not in front of him, and never put your head over the horse's neck or poll when practicing this lesson.

- After your horse learns to lower his head in response to your hand pressure on his poll, ask him to drop his head by using downward pressure on the lead rope instead. Once he gets the idea, don't bore him with constant repetition.

- Be consistent in how you ask your horse to lower his head and in using your pressure until you get results. Always hold the pressure steady until you get some response from your horse. This teaches him to find the release, which, in this case, is to drop his head.

- The secret to this method is to not fight your horse to lower his head and keep it down. Instead, you want him to learn to give to your hand pressure and have the confidence that you won't force down his head.

Better Bridling Techniques

You can create head-shyness problems in a horse through poor handling when you bridle and unbridle him. Even when a horse doesn't fling his head and become head-shy, he might still resent the bridle if you don't put it on and take it off him properly. Here are some bridling techniques you can use.

- Fasten the halter around your horse's neck for safety's sake as you bridle him.

- Place your right hand on the horse's poll to slightly lower his head, just as you learned earlier.

- Hold the bridle in your left hand, with the browband open.

- Reach your right hand between the horse's ears to encourage him to lower his head.

- With your right hand, grasp the crown of the bridle and pull the headstall up and onto the horse's head, but don't insert the bit yet.

- Now put your left thumb into the corner of the horse's mouth to encourage him to open it, and then ease the bit into his mouth.

- With the headstall in your left hand, use your right hand and thumb to bend the horse's right ear forward and put it underneath the headstall. Now put the left ear under the headstall, too.

- Adjust your bridle so that the throatlatch isn't too tight and so that the bit sits in the corners of your horse's mouth. On a young horse, I like the bit to be just a little higher in the corners of his mouth, so that he learns to carry the bit on top of his tongue. As a horse becomes more seasoned, I adjust the bit to sit a little lower in his mouth.

- When unbridling your horse, go slowly and never pull the bit from your horse's mouth. Metal banging against his teeth doesn't leave him with happy thoughts about riding or the bridle. Give him time to "spit out" the bit as you slowly slip off the bridle.

Control the Horse's Body

I work with every horse to control his body from the ground—without ever touching him. I hold the lead rope, but I don't have to put my hand on the horse to get him to move when and where I want.

Much of my groundwork is directed at the horse's hindquarters. Too many people try to control the horse's head and front end without realizing that the hindquarters are an "engine" that drives the horse forward. The front end is just the "steering wheel." If these people can learn how to put the horse's rear end into neutral by controlling the hindquarters, they can take power away from a horse.

About 65 percent of the horse's weight is on his front end, so his hindquarters actually are the easiest part to move if you know what to do. Once you can move and control the hindquarters and the two hind feet, tension and stiffness leave the horse's rib cage, entire front end and, ultimately, the lead rope or rein. Then you have a horse that is soft and supple on the front end, even though you actually worked on the hind end. This is why you don't jerk or pull on the head when trying to soften a horse; the tension you see there actually comes from the horse's hind end and travels forward.

Sound bridling techniques help minimize head-shyness and resentment.

65

To safely control the horse's hindquarters, use an imaginary "V" created by two lines, one drawn from the horse's hip and the other perpendicular to the point of his shoulder.

"Your goal is to get your horse's feet moving without pulling on his head."

I can diagnose a lot of a horse's problems just by working his hind end. Once I can move his hind end freely, I can soften his entire body. This softness is one result of solid groundwork. When the horse resists physically, he's unable to go to the next step, so I must get that softness before I can advance.

Lines of Control

Before learning to control your horse's hindquarters, you need to draw some imaginary boundary lines on your horse's body. These three points help you define your position when working with your horse:

- the point of his shoulder

- the drive-line, right behind the girth area

- his hip and hindquarters

Look at your horse from the side and mentally divide him in two parts. Draw one imaginary vertical line right about where the girth would be. Remember: Any time you are in front of that line, you drive your horse's front end. You drive his hindquarters any time you're behind that line. For example, if you stand in front of the horse's shoulder and move toward him, you drive his front end away from you, and he should turn away. But if you stand at his hip and move toward him, you drive his hindquarters forward.

Control the Hindquarters

Have you ever noticed that some people talk and talk, but don't really communicate anything? You can do this with your horse—talk to him all day long—but if you don't use body language and expression, you

Assertive, emphatic body language and twirling the lead might be required when first teaching a horse to move his hindquarters,

As the horse begins to understand about moving his hindquarters, body language alone might be a sufficient cue to get the desired response.

Ultimately, a glance from a distance should be pressure enough to move the horse's hindquarters.

can't really communicate with him at all. On the other hand, you can say nothing to your horse, but communicate a great deal of information to him.

When it comes to controlling, or yielding your horse's hindquarters, your body language and expression are critical. This is how you communicate to your horse what you expect him to do.

Remember what you learned about handling your lead rope. Your direction hand is always the hand closest to the horse and directs him in the way to go. Your driving hand is closest to the rope's tail end. You drive your horse forward by twirling your rope.

- Before you ask your horse to move his hindquarters, he must be focused on and looking at you. This keeps you safe.

- Imagine two lines in the dirt extending from your horse's side. One line is perpendicular to the point of your horse's

67

Measure from the ground to your waist to determine the approximate amount of lead to twirl in your driving hand.

Use an overhand motion to twirl the tail of the lead and practice twirling with each hand.

shoulder, while the other line comes from his hip to meet the line drawn from his shoulder. The point of this "V," where the two lines meet, is where you stand for safety's sake, not at the point of the shoulder close to the horse, because you don't want your horse to swing his hind end around every time you approach his shoulder. You move very little when you're inside the V.

- Your goal is to get your horse's feet moving without pulling on his head.

- Use your body language with expression and a slight crouch as you step to the V created where the two lines from your horse's hip and shoulder meet. Direct your focus at your horse's hip. You're asking the horse's body to move, which is why you don't focus on his head. Focus on the part of the body you want to move, in this case, the horse's hind end.

- Without pulling on the horse's head with your direction hand, point toward the hindquarters with your driving hand.

- If the horse doesn't move his hind end, lift your driving hand and twirl your rope, starting slowly and accelerating as needed. Remember: Twirl the rope overhand, not underhanded.

- If necessary because your horse doesn't move his hindquarters, hit the ground with the end of the rope.

- If your horse still doesn't move after you've hit the ground with the rope, accelerate your twirling action and, as a last resort, pop his hindquarters with the end of the rope.

- Never pop your horse in front of the hip when trying to move his hindquarters.

- In order to be effective in controlling the hindquarters, you must be assertive. Don't be timid or "pick" at the horse, or he becomes sour and resentful.

- Your horse eventually should move his hind end, stepping to the side, while the front end stays stationary. This not a side-pass because his front end and front feet stay put; the horse basically swings his hindquarters away from you.

- Respond to the slightest try, or effort, your horse makes by relieving pressure from the twirling rope. At first he might move only one hind foot, but he tried. Give him a moment and then resume twirling, keeping your focus on the hip. Focus on the hind end, not the front end, and never fight with your horse by pulling on his head with the lead.

- Once he catches on to the maneuver, let your horse soak a minute or two, so he realizes he's done something right. Watch for him to lick his lips and soften his eye,

which shows he understands and is relaxed with his task.

- When your horse understands that you want him to move his hindquarters, work on controlling the hindquarters from each side. Never work only one side of your horse—always work both sides.

- As your horse picks up on this lesson, he begins to swing his hindquarters when you take a step toward his hip or, ultimately, just look at his hip.

- Keep your lessons short and effective so the horse doesn't get bored. It's important to have rhythm in your body and to stay

The left hand directs the horse to travel to the left as the right hand drives him forward.

To ask the horse to yield his hindquarters, use the right and left hands respectively to direct and drive him to the right.

As the horse travels by, let the lead slide through the directing hand, and then ask the horse to yield his hindquarters and face you.

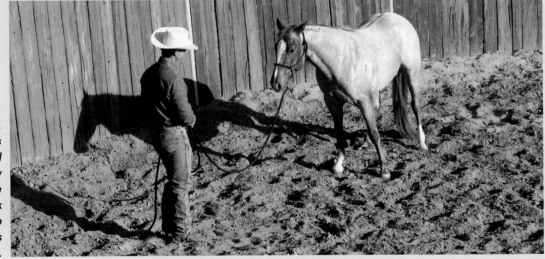

As always, with hands down and relaxed, allow the horse time to soak and absorb what he's learned.

relaxed as you work; don't be stiff or slow with your body language.

- As you progress, you can move faster through this lesson. If your feet move faster, your horse's feet should move faster, and vice versa.

- Define your boundary lines—be persistent and consistent. Any correction should be something the horse can understand. The horse should relate to your body language, not just the rope in your hand.

Direct and Drive

Once you can easily control your horse's hindquarters by having him yield to either side, you are ready to advance and direct and drive your horse. But your horse must clearly understand the first lesson before you move to this next step.

This groundwork lesson teaches the horse to follow your hand and your direction. The lesson also helps the horse learn to follow your lead and make a decision for himself. Because you drive the horse forward, but don't lead him, he must think about moving forward. Again, you want no confrontation on the front end, no pulling on his head.

Feel and timing are important. You use the horse's pressure points to push away his front end and drive his hind end forward. This exercise is useful in many areas and is especially helpful for trailer loading.

The direct-and-drive exercise also is excellent for teaching a horse to respect your space. If your horse crowds too closely to you at any time, drive him away from you by twirling the rope in your driving hand. If you walk out of the horse's space or back away as he gets too close, you teach him to crowd you. Instead of moving your feet, make him move his feet.

- To make this exercise easier on the horse and you, use a fence as a guide, so the horse has a boundary within which to work. Your horse is parallel to the fence, while you face the fence, and direct the horse to drive forward between you and the fence.

- This is not longeing. You don't want the horse to go all the way around you in a circle. You just want him to go straight by you and then turn to face you.

- Stay out and away from your horse as you work. Remember the "V" between his shoulder and hip.

- Lift your directing hand in the direction you want your horse to go.

- Take one step toward your horse's hip.

- Next, pick up your driving hand. If your horse's feet don't move, start twirling your lead rope.

- Keep twirling your lead until your horse makes an effort. Don't quit asking until the horse tries to do what you want. If necessary, keep twirling your rope emphatically and hitting the ground with it until

When tying your horse, take a double wrap around the pipe and bring the tail through a loop to create a quick-release knot.

After the initial quick-release knot is tied, the tail of the lead can be "daisy-chained" repeatedly, yet still be untied quickly.

your horse responds properly. Let the rope slide through your direction hand as he goes by, and then ask him to yield his hindquarters, so that he swings around and faces you once again.

- When he responds correctly, let your horse soak, and during this time keep both your hands down and relaxed. "Hands-down" tells the horse you are relaxed and not expecting anything of him at the moment. If your hands are up, this tells the horse you're about to ask him to do something.

- As your horse catches on to driving and directing, you can narrow the distance between you and the fence so your horse has to move through a smaller space, which makes the lesson more challenging.

Direct and Drive Over an Obstacle

Once your horse is comfortable with the basic direct-and-drive exercise, you can introduce an obstacle for him to cross. This also can help your horse learn to step up and into the trailer and to handle obstacles on the trail. A single pole or rail is a great obstacle to use at first. Lay a pole on the ground perpendicular to the fence, with one end of the pole at the base of the fence.

- Don't lead your horse to the pole. Instead, drive him into position to cross it.

- Lift your direction hand to send him over the pole.

- Your horse might try to avoid the obstacle, but continue to drive him forward.

- Twirl the lead rope as necessary with your driving hand until your horse makes a move to cross over the pole.

- Don't quit driving your horse until he tries to do what you want.

- As soon as your horse tries, stop twirling your rope.

- When your horse has gone over the pole, take a step toward his hindquarters, asking him to yield his hindquarters so that he turns to face you again.

your horse moves forward; be consistent and don't give up.

- Stop twirling as soon as you have any forward movement from your horse. It might take a few tries for him to realize that he's supposed to drive past you and then stop.

- Release or drop your hands as soon as

- Drop your hands and let your horse soak to absorb the lesson, as well as to let him know that what he did was right.

- Be sure to move your horse's hindquarters so that he faces you before driving him over the pole in the other direction.

- Send your horse back and forth over the pole in both directions several times until he is relaxed and matter-of-fact about the obstacle.

- Watch for him to lick his lips, which shows he is accepting and relaxed.

"It's a mistake to think that you've taught your horse to load if you've just walked him onto a trailer one time without problems."

7
TRAILER-LOADING

One of the most common complaints I hear from horse owners is that their horses are difficult or, in some cases, impossible to load. The problem is so widespread that trailer-loading is one of the most popular sessions during my demonstrations at expos and when I'm on tour.

There can be many reasons why a horse doesn't want to load. He might have had a negative experience the first time he set foot in a trailer, and you can be sure that is never forgotten. Some horses become poor loaders because bad

Patience and solid groundwork are keys in teaching a horse to load consistently and well.

Any number of reasons can contribute to trailer-loading difficulties, from an accident or poor driving habits to a lack of experience or instruction.

driving has made them nervous and they dread the ride, or the horse might have experienced an accident in the trailer. Other horses simply never have been taught to load, and when they have to be taken somewhere, they naturally resist out of fear and ignorance.

Whatever the reasons a horse doesn't want to load, invariably the solution points to one thing—groundwork. Any horse that has a problem with trailer-loading is lacking some foundational work on the ground. Once you put those foundation pieces together correctly, even horses that have refused to load can learn to load quietly and easily. A horse might be frightened and lack confidence, but patience and good groundwork take care of these things.

Many horses that I work in trailer-loading demonstrations have a lot more going on than just the fact that they don't want to get in trailers. Some horses have fear issues that must be overcome. There are often respect issues that need to be dealt with, as these horses often walk all over their owners and push them around. This has nothing to do

with the trailer, but surely makes things more difficult once a trailer is in the picture.

It's a mistake to think that you've taught your horse to load if you've walked him onto a trailer only one time without problems. I guarantee: If you don't teach a horse to load consistently and to stand until you ask him to unload, a time will come when he decides he doesn't want to get in that trailer. It's not a matter of if this will happen; it's just a matter of when.

First Things First

If the first time you had to drive a car were because you just cut your arm and had to get to the hospital, that initial driving experience would be a stressful one. And, chances are, you'd think about it every time you got behind the wheel.

It's the same with horses. Don't wait until you need to take your horse somewhere to teach him to load. You'll hurry and end up skipping steps, which shortchanges your horse. Your goal shouldn't be to get the horse in the trailer this one time, but to teach your horse correctly, so he loads every time you ask him.

A horse has an excellent memory, and his survival instincts really seem to hammer home the negative experiences. If his first trailer experience is a bad one, he tends to fret and fight every time you start to load him. On the other hand, if you take the time to teach him how to load and make it a positive thing, he thinks of the trailer as a safe place to be.

There's a very good reason this chapter follows the previous chapter on groundwork. In order to successfully teach your horse to load, you need to have mastered the exercises on controlling the hindquarters and for directing and driving your horse. He also needs to know how to lead well. Everything builds on the steps he's already learned.

Trailer-loading is like any other lesson you teach your horse, although loading is one of the more unnatural things you teach a horse. Your preparation away from the trailer is what gives you success when you do load your horse. You can effectively control and move your horse's hindquarters, and direct and drive him through narrow spaces and over obstacles, such as a pole or log on the ground. You also can drive your horse across a board or wooden bridge. These exercises simulate a narrow trailer door opening and stepping up into a trailer.

By teaching the techniques and introducing such obstacles, your preparation is done, and your tools are in place before you ever

Use body language and a slight crouch when teaching a horse to back, but work from the side, not directly in front of the horse.

77

The horse should back out of my space in response to my body language.

approach the trailer with your horse. It is so important to build these steps in increments and to increase the difficulty gradually. Doing these things builds your horse's confidence without putting too much pressure on him at one time.

Teach the Back First

I am adamant about all my horses knowing how to back out of a trailer. It's much safer for both my horse and me to back him, rather than turn him around and lead him from a trailer. I've seen horses jump on top of their handlers when being led from a trailer, and I've seen situations where someone could not get a horse out because there was no room for him to turn around inside, and he'd never been taught to back from a trailer. Somebody actually had to cut open the trailer just to free the horse.

It's easy to teach your horse to back from the ground. Just remember that you don't want to put pressure on his head. Concentrate

instead on his feet. The head follows once the feet move.

- Keep your horse's head straight with the lead rope, but don't pull or jerk him backward.

- Using your body expression and a slight crouch, approach your horse from the front, but standing to his side. Your body language and expression are important. Use these before you use your rope.

- If the horse doesn't back out of your space as you approach his nose, correct him. Use the end of the lead rope to pop him on the point of his shoulder and drive him back.

- Twirl your rope only as needed to encourage your horse to move backward.

- Quit twirling as soon as your horse takes a step back.

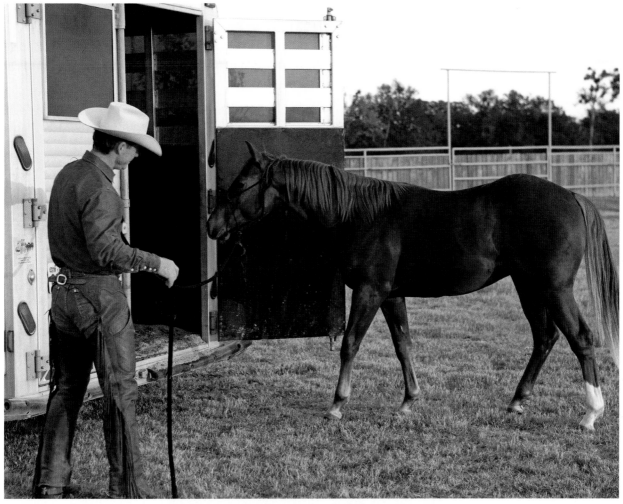

Allow the horse time to look into the trailer and to become comfortable near it.

- Let your horse soak and rest a minute once he backs several steps correctly.

- Only when you can drive back your horse easily should you begin backing him by applying any pressure on the lead rope.

Introduce the Trailer

For trailer-loading, the only equipment I need is my halter and lead. I use the same method whether I work with a weanling that has never seen a trailer or with an older horse that has developed serious loading issues. These techniques work with any horse I need to load.

Before you approach the trailer, first reinforce the basic groundwork exercises with your horse, controlling and yielding his hindquarters, and directing and driving him. The horse needs to learn to pick up his feet and look in the direction he's going, which is why you also want to direct and drive him over an obstacle. Make sure your horse is solid on these exercises and responds well before trying to load him.

Park the trailer in an open area, with doors and windows opened to allow as much light as possible inside. Don't open an escape door, and be sure the windows have bars; you'd be amazed at the small spaces a horse might try to go through. Make sure all trailer doors and dividers are secured so they can't swing, startle or bump the horse. If it's a step-up trailer, try to park on slightly sloping ground to lessen the distance the horse must step up and down during his first loading experience.

Walk your horse to the trailer door, but don't try to pull him closer if he stops, and never walk in front of him, trying to lead him. You drive him into the trailer rather than lead him there.

Use the direct-and-drive exercise to teach your horse to load because this method lets you stay out of the horse's way, which makes

79

loading much safer than it would be otherwise. Directing and driving also makes it the horse's decision to load into the trailer instead of something he is forced to do. It's

"If you pull on his head, the horse resists and transfers his weight to his hind end, just as if he's a seesaw. With weight on the hind end, his feet 'lock up,' and it is difficult to get him to move."

more meaningful to the horse when loading is his idea.

When someone tries to load a horse by leading him, the person ends up pulling on the horse's head. The focus is on the head and front end, but the focus actually should be on driving his hind end forward. If you pull on his head, the horse resists and transfers his weight to his hind end, just as if he's a seesaw. With weight on his hind end, his feet "lock up," and it is difficult to get him to move easily.

When you work with a young horse, or one that has no trailer-loading experience, your goal is to teach him to load and unload properly. If you have an older horse or one that has become a problem loader, you must correct him, as well as teach him the best way to load. This might mean you need to twirl your rope more aggressively at times. Don't despair if your horse seems to get worse

Use the familiar direct-and-drive exercise, which keeps you safely to the side, to encourage the horse to load.

before he gets better. He sometimes has to "backslide" before he improves.

When loading your horse, be consistent with your cues and don't give up. Always end each session on a positive note with the horse accomplishing a task you have asked him to do.

Load Step-by-Step

Don't think of this exercise as loading your horse into the trailer; just think of it as a direct-and-drive exercise and proceed as usual. Don't fight with your horse to load him; instead, direct him and drive him forward into the trailer.

- When loading your horse, he should face the trailer door and stand straight. You stand to the side of the trailer door opening and out of the horse's way.

- Keep your horse's head straight so his focus remains on the trailer. Don't look your horse in the eye; that blocks him from moving forward. Instead, keep your focus on his hip.

- Raise your direction hand to signal your horse that you want him to drive forward, toward the trailer.

- If he doesn't move forward, lift your driving hand and begin twirling the rope. If he backs, which he will, keep twirling to drive him forward.

- Build on every try and progression your horse makes by giving him relief. When the horse tries to move forward, reward him by lowering your hands, so he can relax, and let him soak.

- Ask your horse to drive forward until he is comfortable with his head inside the trailer. Don't get in a hurry. Let your horse drop his head and sniff the trailer. If he doesn't lower his head, he can't be sure where to place his feet. Don't be a dictator telling the horse where to put his feet. Let him make this decision.

- The next step is for your horse to pick up a foot to step into the trailer, so you want him to understand that the release of pressure comes as soon as he picks up a foot. Reward each progression by not

When the horse is allowed to make the decision to step into the trailer, he has a meaningful learning experience.

twirling the rope and dropping your hands to give him relief.

- Don't worry if your horse goes partway into the trailer with only his front end and then backs out of the trailer. He is gaining confidence, so don't try to force him all the way into the trailer. I always prefer that a horse go gradually, step-by-step, and gain the courage to load, rather than jump in the trailer immediately.

Teaching a horse to back out of a trailer is just as important as teaching him to step into one.

- Continue to drive your horse forward. It doesn't take long for him to realize the pressure goes away once he is in the trailer.

- When your horse moves forward and into the trailer, let the lead rope in your direction hand slide. You don't want any pressure on your horse's head to confuse him or to stop him from going forward. This is where the 13-foot lead comes in handy, so use it.

- The first time your horse steps all the way inside the trailer, he might stand there or back out immediately. Either way is fine, but use your lead rope as necessary to keep your horse facing forward when he's in the trailer. Don't let your horse turn around in the trailer and walk out of it, but don't force him to stay inside if he wants to back out of the trailer.

- If your horse immediately backs from the trailer, don't try to force him to stay there. Instead, continue loading him until he realizes it's less work for him to stay inside the trailer and wait until you ask him to back out of it. I'd rather a horse back from the trailer several times than have him freeze and not want to move.

- Don't tie your horse in the trailer the first few times he loads, and don't close the door or dividers.

- Once your horse loads and stands quietly in the trailer, make sure that he knows you are there and, if possible, walk into the trailer beside him. Rub your horse, and let him stand and soak for a few minutes, so he thinks of the trailer as a good place. He always should feel as if the trailer is a place to relax, not work.

- After your horse stands in the trailer a few minutes, ask him to back by driving him, just as you do outside the trailer. Stay in front of and to the side of your horse as you drive him back.

- Be aware that the first time he steps out of the trailer, he might become startled, so don't stand directly in front of him. Encourage him to continue backing all the way out of the trailer the first time you unload him.

- Concentrate on backing your horse slowly and in a relaxed manner. The way he learns to back out of a trailer in the beginning is how he always tries to do it in the future.

- When you've unloaded your horse the first time, let him stand and soak a minute.

- Then ask him to load again, just as you did before. During the initial training session, always load and unload your horse several times. You want him to be very relaxed and comfortable with the entire scenario. If your horse stomps in the trailer or acts up, load and unload him until he finds comfort standing in the trailer.

- As your horse becomes better about loading, you won't even have to twirl your rope. Just raise your direction hand, and your horse steps into the trailer. It's important to escalate your energy and rhythm to encourage movement from your horse. If you don't raise your energy, you desensitize your horse, instead of developing a prompt response.

"... you should never bribe a horse to do something."

- Once you and your horse are comfortable with loading, you can stand farther away from him and to the side. After your horse completely understands about loading through the direct-and-drive method, you can lead him into the trailer if you like. But make very sure he first loads solidly by directing and driving him.

Trailer-Tying and the First Ride

After your horse comfortably loads and unloads, and stands in the trailer until you ask him to back out of it, you can tie him in the trailer. However, you should never tie a horse until you have put the butt bar or chain in place and have closed the divider.

With an inexperienced horse, I always tie the lead shorter rather than longer. As the horse becomes accustomed to trailering, I tie him out a little longer, but I never leave a horse loose in the trailer. A horse can keep his footing better with his head and neck up. Also, some horses lower their heads and might even try to get under a divider, so it's safer to restrain a horse by tying him.

I use a quick-release knot so I can get it undone easily under pressure, and make sure the rope tail doesn't hang down and around my horse's legs, where the lead rope might startle him.

It's worth mentioning here: Every horse owner should carry a pocketknife at all times. In an emergency you might need to cut a horse loose, and that's no time to run looking for a knife or tool to free him.

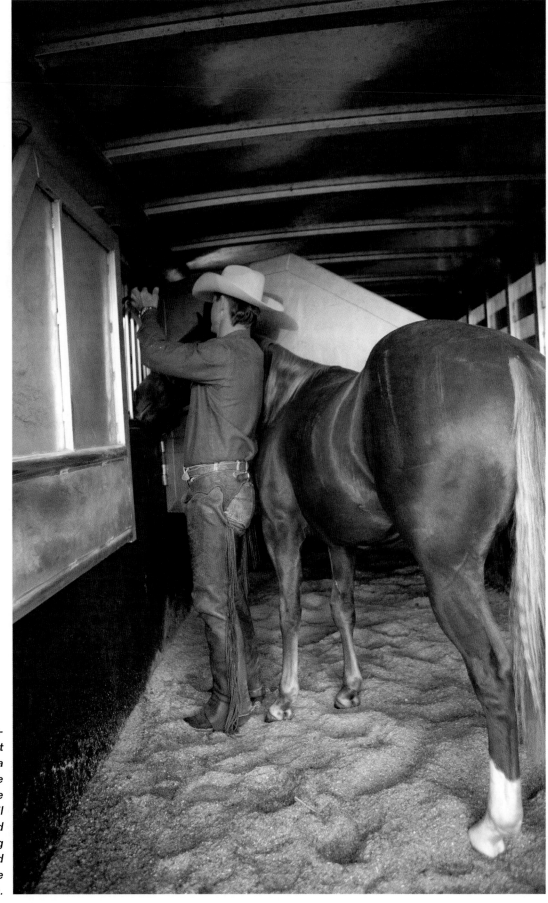

Use a quick-release knot when tying a horse in the trailer, and be sure the tail of the lead doesn't hang down and around the horse's legs.

Practically Speaking: Treats and Trailers

Horse owners often think they can use treats or feed to lure horses into the trailer. I am against this practice for several reasons.

One, you should never bribe a horse to do something. If you start by bribing him, he always expects a treat and becomes resentful and sullen when you don't give him what he wants.

Two, if the horse is focused on getting to feed, his focus is not on the trailer. You want him to pay attention to you and to the trailer—nothing else.

Finally, horses can be anxious about learning to load, which can cause them to gobble and bolt down feed or hay once they're in the trailer. That might lead to colic, so the best bet is never to feed a horse when teaching him to load.

Even with my experienced, quiet loaders, I don't give the horses any hay or feed until we've been on the road a little while.

The first time your horse travels in the trailer, go on just a short ride. Ten minutes or so is plenty. Afterward, unload and put up your horse or turn him loose. Don't reload him again after the first ride. You want to end his ride on a pleasant note and keep things nice and easy.

I can't talk about trailer-loading without mentioning the importance of good hauling habits. You can have a horse that loads great, but ruin him with bad hauling. If you ever have ridden in a horse trailer, you have a much greater appreciation for what the horse undergoes.

Remember: You might know when you're about to hit the brakes and slow down, but your horse doesn't. Be gradual with both acceleration and braking, so your horse can brace himself and not feel like he has to scramble to keep his footing. Make wide turns so your horse isn't thrown off-balance.

Be sure your trailer is a comfortable place for your horse. Use non-slip rubber mats that provide good traction and cushion. Even in cold weather, there should be plenty of ventilation and moving air. Hauling in a warm, enclosed trailer is just asking for respiratory problems. Only use leg wraps or leg protection if your horse is used to those. A trailer ride isn't the first time your horse should be introduced to something on his legs; that only causes him more stress.

I give electrolyte paste to all my horses before we hit the road. This encourages them to drink and stay hydrated. By using paste, instead of powdered electrolytes that I add to water, I know the horses get the amount of electrolytes they need.

On trips longer than four hours, I'm sure to stop and offer water to my horses. A lot of horses won't drink while a trailer is moving, even with a water bucket hanging in front of them. I always try to stop in the shade and give the horses a break from travel to encourage them to drink before getting on the road again. If possible, I bring water from home and always offer water in a bucket familiar to the horse. Keeping horses hydrated while traveling is essential, especially on long trips.

"Many problems people experience with their horses stem from the fact that the people are not balanced correctly in their saddles."

8

THE LOWER HALF

When someone shops for a horse, one of the things he looks for is a well-built, well-balanced individual. The irony is that an unbalanced rider can negatively affect a beautifully balanced, athletic horse.

I've found that frequently when a rider complains of a sore back, it's due to the way he rides, not the fact that he has a rough horse. Many problems people experience with their horses stem from the fact that the people are not balanced correctly in their saddles to effectively maneuver their horses..

If you are out of balance in the saddle, you also are going

Leg position 3, for example, and seat position 2 are used to move the horse's hindquarters.

to be out of time and rhythm with your horse's movements. On the other hand, when you are balanced in the saddle, you can better help your horse remain balanced as you ride.

"Too many people ride their saddles, not their horses."

One common problem I see: People try to work on maneuvers when they're off balance and out of time with their horses. Being an unbalanced rider makes it twice as hard for a horse to understand what the rider asks him to do. A balanced rider stays out of his horse's way and moves with his horse's flow and stride. When a rider is balanced in the saddle, he can better feel his horse's footfall underneath, and this makes it easier to pick up the correct lead or do various maneuvers.

Many people are under the impression a rider just sits on a horse. But you really need to actively move your hips in rhythm with the horse's motion. Your hips should move and your lower back should roll slightly; you don't want to stiffen your back. If you don't move in sync with your horse's rhythmic motion, you start bouncing in the saddle, and this makes for a rough ride, as well as throwing you off balance. When your hips move in rhythm with the horse, you have a much more comfortable ride since your hips can absorb the shock.

Although your hips should work in a forward-and-back motion with your horse's movement, your upper body should remain still. Your shoulders always should be square and in line with your horse's shoulders. Many riders unconsciously twist their shoulders to one side. Doing this can twist your seat in the saddle and immediately put you off balance. Men often ride with a wallet in a back pocket, but even this can offset a rider's balance, so leave the billfold at home.

Remember to be conscious of your breathing when you ride, and make it a point to breathe naturally. If you breathe shallowly or hold your breath, your body tenses, affecting both your balance and position. On the other hand, breathing deeply allows you to have a deeper seat in the saddle and to relax into your horse's movements.

One of the big mistakes I see in the horse industry: A person—before he's an accomplished rider—tries to train his horse. You must be able to ride comfortably, in balance and rhythm with your horse, before you try to teach maneuvers. You must be a good rider before you can be a trainer. You can't expect to perform advanced maneuvers on a horse if you don't have correct, centered balance.

Learning to ride correctly is so important. It takes time and practice to improve your timing and skill in the saddle. Your position in the saddle has a great deal to do with riding correctly. One of the things I admire about the English horse world is that riders are taught riding principles and the importance of correct position from day one. Position alone isn't a substitute for horsemanship, but definitely is a big part of becoming a better horseman or -woman.

Seat Position

Your seat position influences your balance in the saddle. You can find your natural balance through proper seat position. This

In seat position 1, the rider's body is forward in the saddle, which encourages faster, forward motion from the horse.

Practically Speaking: Your Saddle Influences Your Position

Your saddle greatly influences your seat position. There should be enough room in the saddle seat for you to maneuver into the different seat positions.

The lowest part of the saddle seat should be in the middle, from front to back, so you can take a centered seat position 2. The flatter and lower the saddle seat, the better you feel your horse and communicate with him; this is why I don't like a lot of buildup in my saddle seat.

means you can't be only a passenger, but constantly must readjust your hip movements to the horse's movements as you ride. If you ride still and stiffly, the horse's power quickly throws you off balance.

Too many people ride their saddles, not their horses. In other words, people push their bodies back against the cantles and shove their legs forward in the stirrups, with their knees locked.

Riding that way puts you off balance and behind your horse's forward movement. You can't move properly with your horse when you're in this position. You should sit centered in the saddle, and your weight should be distributed through your seat, not braced with your legs.

Your seat is your greatest aid in communicating with your horse. Using your seat effectively can keep you from overusing your reins. Depending on where you sit in the saddle, you send your horse different messages. Unless you specifically ask your horse for a change, you should sit on your seat bones, not rocked back on your pockets.

As you begin refining your horsemanship, your first cue—whether you stop, slow or turn your horse—always should come from your seat and then travel down and through the legs. Your hands always should give the lightest of your cues. Become more aware of how you cue your horse, so you can create good riding habits. Then it becomes second nature for you to use the correct technique.

Each of the following three seat positions you take in your saddle means a different thing to your horse:

People most often ride in the centered seat position 2 when they're on "cruise control" and not asking their horses to change gait or direction.

Seat position 3 is used for stopping and backing a horse as the rider softens his lower back and rolls off his seat bones and onto his "pockets."

Seat position 1: Slide forward so you sit toward the front of the saddle. This position encourages faster forward movement from your horse. Think of a jockey; he rides far forward on his horse, asking for forward movement and freeing the horse's hindquarters.

Seat position 2: The center of the saddle is where you should ride when you aren't asking your horse for a change in pace or direction. Most riding is done in this position. Think of seat position 2 as "cruise control."

Seat position 3: The third position, toward the back of the saddle and against the cantle, is used for stopping or backing your horse. You simply move off your seat bones and roll your behind against the cantle, just as if you're riding a Harley. As soon as the horse responds, roll up to seat position 2 and onto your seat bones again. Don't make a habit of riding in seat position 3 because the horse's kidneys and loin are right in this area and can become sore and irritated if you ride in this position all the time.

There also are three relative seat positions from side to side in the saddle. Depending on what you ask your horse to do, you might sit on your left seat bone, your right seat bone, or on both seat bones in the middle of your saddle, the centered position. Unless you specifically direct your horse for sideways movement, you usually sit centered on both seat bones in the middle position.

Leg Position

Many riders make the mistake of constantly gripping with the lower legs, which actually signals a horse to accelerate. Ironically, such a rider starts losing his balance as soon as he tries, with his lower legs, to hold onto his horse. The rider gripping with his lower legs actually pushes himself forward in the saddle and out of rhythm with his horse's motion.

Your leg from the knee down should be used only to communicate with the horse—not to hold onto your horse. From the knees down, keep your legs away from your horse's

In position 1, the leg lies forward along the girth line and is used there to move the horse's shoulders and his front end.

Leg position 2, where the leg rests unless the rider gives a specific cue, also can be used to move the horse's entire body

In position 3 the leg is in the back cinch area and is used to move the horse's hind end.

sides unless you are giving a specific cue or request. Otherwise, your legs should rest softly against your horse's sides, without any pressure.

"With your leg, there are three ways to ask your horse for a response."

Grip your horse from your knees up, engaging the muscles through your inseam up to the groin area. Don't pick at your horse by using your legs more than you need, which ends up having the opposite effect from what you want. If you continue to kick your horse or persist in gripping with your lower legs, you desensitize him—when he already is responding to what you have asked him to do.

As with saddle position, there are three leg positions you use when riding horseback.

Leg position 1: Your legs are against your horse's sides as close to the girth as possible. In this position, your legs move your horse's shoulders and his front end.

Leg position 2: Your legs are behind the front girth, between the front and back girths and just a few inches behind leg position 1. Leg position 2 allows you to move the horse's entire body. As with seat position 2, leg position 2 is where your leg should be unless you are giving a specific cue.

Leg position 3: Your legs are at the back girth area, several inches behind position 2. A leg in position 3 moves the horse's hind end.

Always introduce leg position 3 to your horse first because this position is used to move his hind end, the lightest and easiest part of the horse to move. Once you can move the hind end, use leg position 1 to move your horse's front end. Only after your horse is soft and supple, and understands what you ask with leg positions 1 and 3, do you introduce leg position 2, which allows you to move your horse's entire body.

Adjust your stirrups so you have a good bend to your knee. If your stirrups are too long, it is hard to cue the horse with your leg. When you use your legs to ask your horse to move, always ask with pulsating pressure—press and release. Don't maintain constant pressure; doing so only encourages your horse to lean on your legs. As soon as he responds, release your leg pressure.

With your leg, there are three ways to ask your horse for a response. Always ask first with the most subtle cue, then increase intensity only if your horse doesn't respond. First, turn out your toe and squeeze with your calf. If your horse doesn't respond, then bump his side with your leg. If the bump doesn't bring the response, then pick up your leg, lifting it away from the horse's side, and kick with your heel. Only after you have asked in this 1-2-3-sequence and not gotten a correct response from the horse should you proceed to use your crop, the end of your reins or your mecate to reinforce the leg cue.

Posting

Contrary to what you might think, posting isn't only for riders in English saddles. I routinely recommend posting to help riders learn to find a centered seat in position 2 and to work on their balance.

Posting helps you understand your horse's footfall because you post in rhythm with his stride and movement as you rise and fall in the saddle to his footfall. Riders who have

"... your feet anchor your balance, which is why their position is so important."

a hard time with lead changes benefit from posting exercise.

For starters, realize that your feet anchor your balance, which is why their position is so important. If your feet are too far back, they throw your body forward. If the feet are too forward, they shift your body back. Either way, you're out of balance.

To maintain centered balance, your legs should be underneath you, so that your heels are in line with your hips. If someone looks at your horse from the side, that person should be able to draw an imaginary line straight down from your hips to touch your heels.

Be sure that neither foot is pushed all the way to the heel into your stirrup. If your entire foot is in the stirrup, your toes point down and your heel comes up. This tilts your body forward, putting you off balance and causing you to grip with your lower legs. Instead, keep your heels down and the balls of your feet resting in the center of the

With only the toes of his feet in the stirrups, a rider can't maintain proper balance, especially when posting.

When the entire foot is in the stirrup, the toes tend to point down and the heel rises, which tilts the rider forward and out of balance with his horse.

Correctly positioning the balls of the feet on the stirrup treads is important because the rider's feet anchor his balance.

stirrup treads. You can't post if your feet aren't in the correct position.

"He [your horse] already should understand and respect leg pressure before you ever put on a pair of spurs."

Before you start posting at a trot, begin at a standstill, then try posting at a walk in time with the horse's pace, to find your rhythm and balance. Your legs should remain underneath your body, but as you rise at the post, your hips move forward. Come down in the saddle softly; just touch the saddle, don't slam down against it. All your weight should not hit your horse's back when you post; use your feet to support your body weight.

Riding with Spurs

Many people want to ride with spurs, but spurs are not necessary to become a good rider. Used correctly, spurs can be very helpful aids for correction and in refining your aids, but be aware that you can either help or hurt your horse by riding with spurs. Spurs should be used for refining maneuvers and encouraging your horse, not as weapons or to discourage him.

Here are some tips for using your spurs effectively.

- You must know how to successfully use your legs in all three positions above before you ride with spurs. Proper leg position is important when using spurs. Always keep your toes up and the balls of your feet on the stirrup treads, so you don't use your spurs unintentionally. Relax your legs; if all your weight is in your stirrups, you can't use your spurs effectively.

- Never use spurs to teach a young or green horse to move away from your legs. He already should understand and respect leg pressure before you ever put on a pair of spurs.

- When used improperly, spurs can desensitize a horse and make him so "spur- bound" that he no longer responds to your legs. To be effective, the spur should be the last reinforcement when it comes to communicating with your horse.

- The only time you might use your spurs immediately: When your horse does something dangerous, such as kicking, biting, bucking or lunging, he might hurt you, another person or another horse.

- Except in a dangerous situation, always give your horse the opportunity to respond to your leg before resorting to spurs. Initially squeeze your horse's side with your calf. If he doesn't respond to the squeeze, bump him with your leg, and then kick if your horse still doesn't respond. Only after first using these three cues should you ask with your spurs. So give your leg cues in this order: Squeeze with the calf, bump with your leg, and then kick, and only when there's no response to these requests should you use your spurs.

- A spur is simply a tool to reinforce the suggestion; so never ask first with the spur. When you must use spurs as reinforcement, use them in a downward motion against your horse's sides; don't jab him. Release the spur pressure as soon as your horse responds to your cue. Don't continue holding your spurs against your horse's sides, and don't keep poking your horse with your spurs.

- Once your horse responds and moves the way you want, release the pressure. If you keep your leg or spur pressure on him, he starts to lean on you or push against your legs. Horses lean into pressure, so remember to press and release, or pulsate, instead of maintaining constant pressure with your legs or spurs.

Practically Speaking: Where's Your Focus?

Your visual focus has a great deal to do with your balance. Whenever you ride, your eyes should be focused in the direction you want to go. Our human bodies have a tendency to go in the direction we look; we've been doing that since we were babies first learning to walk, and this translates to riding, as well. Think of riding the way you think about driving a car. If you drive along looking at the radio, the dashboard, or something to the side, sooner or later—probably sooner—you run off the road.

You can tell a lot about a rider's confidence by watching his eyes; if his eyes focus downward, the rider usually lacks confidence. When you look down while riding, you automatically guide your body position in that direction, which causes you to lose your balance and rhythm. Looking at the ground also tells the horse that you are uncertain and lack direction. Focus in the direction you want to go.

Here's another reason not to look down at your horse while you ride. Because of the way your horse's eyes are placed on his head, he easily can tell if you are looking at him. When you look down, he thinks he's either in trouble or doing something wrong.

"Once the horse learns to give his head vertically and carry his head in a natural head-set when you pick up the reins, he doesn't push against the bit when you travel along or do maneuvers."

9

CREATE A NATURAL HEAD-SET

Watch a group of horses running and playing in the pasture, and you're sure to see them carrying their heads in many different ways. Every horse has a slightly different style of carrying himself. His conformation and the way his neck ties in at the withers definitely affect his natural head-set. That's why some horses naturally carry their heads higher or lower than others.

When I talk about creating a natural head-set, I am referring to building a habit, so that the horse automatically gives vertically when I pick up the reins. I want him to flex at the

When I pick up the reins, my horse flexes at the poll and carries his head on the vertical, the result of consistently working to form a good habit.

poll and to carry his head so that, when viewed from the side, his head is vertical, straight up and down. I don't want his nose tucked to his chest, and I don't want it pushing forward. When I release the reins, the horse knows he can relax and release that vertical flexion.

The horse either gives to the bit or pushes against it. Once he learns to give his head vertically and carry his head in a natural head-set when you pick up the reins, he doesn't push against the bit when you travel along or do maneuvers. When a horse pushes against the bit, he hollows his back and becomes stiff throughout his entire body, and you can say goodbye to smoothness and harmony while you're riding.

We all see unnaturally high and low head carriages in certain show-ring competitions, and a rider teaching a horse where to carry his head directly causes such carriage. Personally, I don't like to see a horse moving along with his neck downhill from his withers and his head at knee level. But I do know exactly how a rider gets a horse to maintain this position. The horse learns to carry his head where he finds that "sweet spot" of release from pressure.

Teaching the horse lateral, or side-to-side, and vertical flexion is crucial to creating the natural head-set, riding with balance, and eventually riding with collection. People have tack rooms full of devices to help hold down horses' heads or bend the horses' heads to either side.

But teaching the horse to respond to pressure is all about horsemanship, not mechanics. I don't believe in tying a horse's head to the side for lateral flexion or tying down his head for vertical flexion because there is no release of pressure when the horse gives. I need to be the one helping the horse by immediately releasing the pressure when he gives.

To teach lateral and vertical flexion, you don't need anything but knowledge and patience. In the beginning, never do these lessons in anything but a snaffle bit. The keys are your timing and skill, not a strong bit. As your horse progresses and matures through these lessons, you can advance to a shanked bit.

Rein Management

You can't begin teaching lateral or vertical flexion until you have mastered rein

When using a single sport rein, "choke" down on it as you twist the rein to make a loop.

management. I can't stress enough how important it is to practice rein management. Reins are tools of the trade, and the more comfortable you are handling your reins, the better you can do the following exercises, which are so fundamental to your horse's training.

In the beginning, I suggest using a sport rein, or single rope rein, simply because this is easier to handle than split reins. English-style reins with a buckle in the middle also are helpful for learning rein management.

• The first step is to find the middle of your reins, which is the buckle if you ride with English reins. With rope reins, you might find it helpful to put a piece of tape or mark the center so you can find the middle quickly.

• Sit in seat position 2, the centered seat position, for rein management, with your arms and hands forward. It's important to keep your arms straight and forward

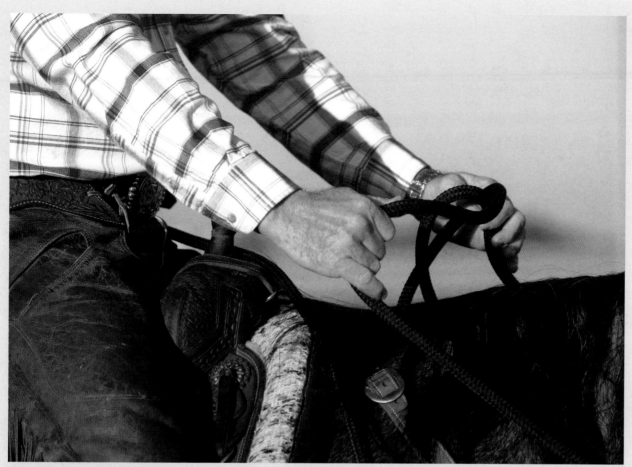

Hold the rein and loop with two hands to create a "bridge" between your hands.

with your elbows locked. If you don't start in this position, you end up with your arms behind your body, which shifts your body forward, throwing off your balance.

- With your left hand, pick up in the middle of your reins and extend your arm all the way forward.

- "Choke" the rein by sliding your right hand all the way down the rein to the top of your horse's neck.

- Using your left hand, twist the rein to the left, to make a loop in your rein, and let any slack in your rein fall to the left side of your horse's neck.

- Now reach to hold your rein with both of your hands.

- Create a rein "bridge" between your hands and put the rein loop in your left hand. Work with both hands on the reins in the

When your arms aren't straight and forward, they eventually end up behind your body, which throws you off balance.

To steady your hand when working on lateral flexion, put it on your leg.

Pulling high with your rein hand, when flexing your horse laterally, can throw him off balance.

flexion exercises. The bridge functions somewhat like training wheels on a bike and lets you know where your hands are. You can widen or shorten the bridge by sliding your hands along the rein.

"The more pressure you put on a horse's mouth, the more you give him something to fight."

- Keep in mind: Although you use your arms and hands in rein management, the majority of pressure is applied through your body and seat—not your hands. The more pressure you put on a horse's mouth, the more you give him something to fight. Pressure on the horse's mouth has the

opposite effect you might think and actually causes him to speed up instead of slow down or stop.

- Use your body to move your arms, instead of bending your elbows to move your arms. When your arms are held straight and forward, you can roll backward or forward on your seat bones to move your arms. Moving the entire body this way, instead of bending only your arms, helps you stay balanced and stable. You have more strength and stability, and can more easily give to the horse when he gives to you. You also can sit deeper into the saddle when preparing for the back, stop or collection.

- Use your arms and hands to create a "hold" on your horse's mouth, not a pull. Think of how it feels when someone puts a hand on your shoulder. He doesn't pull or push you, but just holds you. If you try to move away, you feel the pressure of the hold. If

Pulling your hand behind your hip for lateral flexion throws you off balance in the saddle.

realize: Riding on a tight rein eventually desensitizes the horse.

Once you learn lateral flexion, you realize that you can ride on a loose rein and, if need be, gain immediate control by bending your horse laterally. You can get much more response by pulling on one rein than by pulling on two, which is why I teach lateral flexion before vertical flexion.

Your horse must learn lateral flexion before he can be successful at vertical flexion. It's important to note that your horse's entire body should be involved, not just his head and neck. His body should bend in an arc to follow his nose around laterally. Some horses "rubberneck," meaning their necks bend, but their bodies stay stiff. In some cases, horse even run sideways with their heads held to the side, but this is not lateral flexion.

You can practice lateral flexion on the ground first, by having someone hold your bridle, or by practicing with your bridle hung over a chair. Every position of your hands should mean something to your horse, and the idea is to develop smooth and fluid rein management before actually working with your horse. Once you learn to manage your reins and achieve lateral flexion, you can safely stop and control your horse.

Here's how to develop lateral flexion with your horse.

you move toward the person, the pressure is gone. Use this same technique to create a hold on your horse's mouth with your reins. When your horse gives his head to you, the pressure is gone. That's what you try to accomplish with the hold. Never pull your horse's head; simply hold his mouth until he gives.

Lateral Flexion

You soon discover that lateral flexion gives you a great deal of control of your horse. You can quickly interrupt the horse's forward motion by bringing his nose to the side. Lateral flexion allows you to stop the horse quickly and regain control. In fact, I never stop a horse with both reins, or hands, until he gives laterally and stops well with one rein or one hand.

Too many people ride with tight reins all the time because they are afraid they can't control their horses. What these people don't

- Hold the center of your rein in the left hand, as described previously, and use your right hand to choke the rein all the way down to your horse's neck.

- Now drop your left hand to the horse's withers and hold the rein with both hands.

- Without bending your elbow, go wide with your left hand so that your horse's neck bends around and toward your left hand. Keep your left hand low and level. If your hand is high, you can throw off the horse's balance. Never pull the rein past your hip because this throws you off balance in the saddle. Instead, if you need to steady your left hand, put it on your leg.

- If your horse walks in a circle, maintain a steady hold on the left rein until your horse stands still and gives his head with slack in the rein. When he does, immediately release your hold by opening your left hand and dropping the rein. Don't move your hand forward to release the hold. Remember: You hold; you don't pull. The secret is releasing as soon as your horse gives. Your horse must stand still, not spin or move. Don't release until he is still.

• Now reverse the process to flex your horse laterally to the right. Practice lateral flexion on both sides so your horse bends equally well in either direction.

Vertical Flexion

At one point in my career, I started quite a few young Thoroughbreds and, as with all my horses, I taught them vertical flexion so they gave their heads when I picked up the reins. I quickly found, when these horses went on to race training, that exercise riders didn't appreciate that. Race riders don't want horses to give and be soft; the track riders want horses to be "chargey" and pull against the reins when riders pick up on them. Obviously, this is not the response we want with pleasure or performance horses.

When I pick up the reins with both hands, I expect my horse to give vertically and be soft in hand. Once the horse learns vertical flexion, he automatically puts his head where I've taught him as soon as I pick up both reins.

This vertical flexion routine is one of the most important foundation exercises you can do with your horse. When you ride, your reins should be either loose with your horse moving along naturally, or your reins should be collected with the horse soft and giving his

To ask for vertical flexion, create a "block" with the reins and hold it until your horse responds and becomes soft in hand.

The horse should soften through the neck and flex his head vertically in response to the rein brace.

head vertically. Don't hold onto your horse's mouth without expecting softness; doing otherwise causes him to become resistant and push against your hands.

Here's how to achieve vertical flexion.

- Sitting centered in seat position 2, pick up your reins with both hands and make a bridge as you learned earlier. As you teach your horse vertical flexion, it is important to keep the bridge wide between your hands. Practice sliding your hands as necessary to adjust the bridge's width. Wrap your hands over the top of the reins, not underneath, and around them.

- Hold the reins in a brace in front of the saddle, right above your horse's shoulders. As you hold the brace, remember to keep your arms straight and forward with your elbows locked, but don't pull on the reins. If you pull, you confuse your horse. In teaching lateral flexion, you create a hold with one rein. In vertical flexion, you create a brace with both reins and hold that brace steady until your horse gives. Again, you don't pull, but hold.

- Without pulling, hold the brace steady until your horse gives his head in the vertical position you want, and there is slack in the reins. Then immediately release the hold by opening your hands, which gives instant relief from pressure.

- Don't release your hold, or brace, if your horse tosses his head or is stiff. If you release at either of these times, you create

An overflexed horse's head falls behind the vertical as his chin drops back close to his chest.

When a horse understands vertical flexion, he can learn to back in response to the rider's weight shifting back in the saddle to position 3.

a bad habit by relieving the pressure for the wrong response. Give a prompt release as soon as the horse softens and becomes supple, but not until he does. Releasing when he is stiff and resistant only promotes stiffness throughout his entire body.

• A horse often tries to back when you first ask for vertical flexion because he doesn't understand what you want. If your horse backs, maintain the brace. Let him back to a fence if necessary, but don't release when he backs, or you confuse him.

• Your ultimate goal is for your horse to give vertically as soon as you pick up your reins. His feet and body should be still. You soon establish a habit with which your horse can be comfortable, and create a program so he clearly understands where you want his head. Vertical flexion is like putting in the

clutch in a vehicle. It puts the horse in "neutral" and softens his entire body.

• Once your horse understands vertical flexion, you can hold him in that flexed position longer, which is exactly what you do when you ride with collection. But in the learning stages, don't ask him to hold that flexion for long. As he learns, let him vary between riding with vertical flexion and traveling with his head in a natural position.

Teach the Back

Vertical flexion is a lesson your horse must learn before you ask for the back, and he needs to learn to back before you can expect him to stop well. The stop really is only a reinforcement of the back, which is why you need to master the back first.

Whether you ride for performance or pleasure, whatever the discipline, you want your horse soft and responsive to your body cues. You don't want him to fight or lean on you. Teaching vertical flexion and how to back keeps his response soft.

Your first and main cue in asking for the back is with your seat, not your hands. Your seat responds to the horse's motions, and your hands and arms are the last things to cue your horse to back, and then only because your seat has moved back in the saddle, which moves your upper body, including your arms and back. Your seat, body, arms and hands all work together in the same motion.

By breaking the backing lesson into steps, you can clearly show your horse what you want him to do. These steps are the same whether you teach a young horse or reschool an older horse.

- In seat position 2, ask your horse for vertical flexion.

- Push down with your heels, exhale deeply and roll off your seat bones and onto your behind as you sit deeply into seat position 3 toward the rear of your saddle.

- Keep your arms straight and forward. Your arms move back only because your body moves back, not because you bend your elbows.

- As soon as your horse gives and his feet step backward, roll up and into seat position 2, and open your hands. Don't release your hands when you are in seat position 3.

- After your horse backs and you return to seat position 2, don't release the reins until your horse is soft at the poll with vertical flexion. Your horse learns that he can stop backing once you move back into seat position 2, but he must still maintain vertical flexion to get that release. He must give to the reins before you release your body and open your hands.

- As soon as your horse accomplishes the lesson, let him relax and soak a minute.

- Work in stages and ask your horse to back only a couple of steps at first. Once he

understands what you are asking through your body position, you can back him much farther, but you must continually give a release of pressure as your horse backs.

- In the learning phase, some horses are tougher to back than others. For this type of horse, forcefully use your entire body to move back into seat position 3. Again, you want your horse to back because of your seat position, not because you haul on his mouth with your hands.

Teach the Stop

Because you teach a horse in increments, he needs to fully understand and accomplish each progressive step before you ask him to move to the next one. Skipping steps or rushing ahead only leaves gaps in his performance later. Master the backing exercise before you start working on the stop.

"The stop always should be a reward for the horse."

Make sure your horse backs easily and lightly, and also can back quickly, or he won't respond properly when you begin teaching him to stop. Just as with the back, the stop always starts with your seat, not your hands. Using your seat helps your horse put his body in position to stop, as opposed to you pulling on the bit in his mouth, which doesn't help the horse find the correct body position.

Follow these steps to teach your horse how to stop softly and easily.

- Exhale deeply.

- Roll back into seat position 3 so you are sitting on your behind, not your seat bones.

- Soften your back so you sit deeply into the saddle in position 3.

- Keep your heels down.

- As you ask your horse for the stop, follow through by holding a brace with your arms straight. Don't bend your elbows and pull

By mastering vertical flexion and the back, a horse has the foundation to stop softly and easily, even when cantering.

An easy stop always starts with the rider's seat position and doesn't require him to pull on the reins.

Asking the horse to stop first with your hands, before asking him with your seat, puts weight on the horse's front end, not his hindquarters.

Practically Speaking: Give Physically and Mentally

Sometimes a horse gives his head, and when you release, he immediately pulls his head away. When a horse does this, he is giving physically, but not mentally. This is actually a sign of disrespect.

When that happens, I flex the horse laterally back and forth, from side to side, to soften him mentally and physically. It's critical that the horse learn to give mentally, not just resign himself to giving the minimal physical response he can get away with. I look for willingness, not resignation.

back on the bit. With some horses, you must really use your entire body to emphasize the stop cue.

- When your horse stops, don't let go of the brace until he gives with vertical flexion.

- Let your horse relax and soak a few minutes after the stop. The stop should always be a reward for the horse. Loosen the reins after stopping and while your horse soaks.

- If your horse begins to walk forward before you cue him, back him several steps. Do this as many times as necessary for him to learn that he should stand quietly after stopping until you ask him to move forward. If you try to keep him from walking off by holding a tight rein, you teach him only to resist. Use the skills you've learned to keep him soft and responsive.

- Ask for the stop first at a walk because your horse must learn to get his feet underneath him and into position to stop. Let him get comfortable with this before you ask him to stop at faster gaits.

- When teaching the stop, don't just pull your horse into the ground. At first, it takes a few feet for your horse to come to a full stop. In the beginning, you want a smooth, shuffling three- or four-step stop. Then as your horse learns, shorten this to a stop of just a couple steps. With time, you will develop a crisp, sharp stop as the horse progresses.

10

LEG-YIELDING EXERCISES WITH POSITIONS 3 AND 1

Leg-yielding exercises are excellent ways to teach a horse to become more supple and responsive to a rider's legs when they are used in the three positions described in Chapter 8. Leg-yielding is important for numerous maneuvers, including lead changes, turnarounds, side-passes, two-tracking, counter-bending and opening gates on horseback, as well as controlling the horse's body straightness. I probably use leg-yielding exercises more than any other exercises in my program because I want my horse to respect my legs at all times.

When you're in the saddle, your horse disrespecting your legs is the same as your horse disrespecting and running over

Opening a gate is only one of many maneuvers made easy by training a horse to yield to pressure from his rider's legs.

Leg position 3 is used to control the horse's hindquarters.

you when you're on the ground. A horse that fights your legs is worse, it seems, than one that fights your hands because his entire body pushes on you when he resists pressure from your legs.

Because I use a step-by-step program to build a solid foundation, I introduce leg-yielding to the horse in three sections, starting with the hind end first, which is controlled by leg position 3, as described in Chapter 8. Then I move to leg position 1, which controls the horse's front end. I save leg position 2, which controls the horse's entire body, for last because, before I can advance to leg position 2, the horse must clearly understand what I ask when my legs are in positions 3 and 1.

Leg-Yield the Hindquarters

You've already learned that the hindquarters are the easiest part of the horse to move on the ground because the hind end bears less weight than the front end. The same holds true when you're in the saddle. This is why the first leg-yielding exercise I always teach is moving the horse's hindquarters by using my legs in position 3. The object in yielding the hindquarters is for the horse to pivot on his front feet, so they stay in one place as his hind end swings around his forehand.

Here's how to use a mecate, if necessary, to reinforce the request that your horse yield to pressure from your leg in position 3.

Being able to control the hind end effectively gives you immediate control if your horse acts up or starts to run. You can get lateral flexion by bringing your horse's nose around to the side and using leg position 3 to kick your horse's hind end "out of gear." By swinging around his hindquarters, you take away your horse's power.

Being able to control your horse's hindquarters also can unlock tension in his body, making him soft and responsive. This is why you work on controlling his hind end so much in the beginning. Controlling the hindquarters also keeps you from pulling on your horse's head and mouth with the bit.

Your horse can relax his head and neck when he's not worried about his face being pulled on by your hands. Many people pull with their hands, trying to control the horse's head and front end, but front-end relaxation comes only after the rest of the horse's body has relaxed.

Leg position 3 allows you to bend, supple and relax your horse's body. If you have trouble getting impulsion, or if a horse is dull about responding to your leg, this exercise to move the horse off your leg in position 3 is ideal. Not only does your horse become more responsive to your leg, but the exercise also helps your horse gain impulsion and forward movement.

Every horse can yield his hindquarters if properly asked.

- First, flex your horse laterally, with his nose bent in the same direction as the leg with which you plan to cue him to yield his hindquarters. For example, flex his nose left when using your left leg to move his hindquarters to the right. Ask for this lateral softness at a standstill, just as you learned in Chapter 8, before you put your leg into position 3.

"The less you use your reins, the more your horse relaxes and uses his body."

- Don't ask for lateral softness at the same time you apply leg pressure because your horse then thinks he's supposed to move his hindquarters every time you ask him to give laterally to you. Make sure your cue for lateral softness comes first and then give the leg cue only when you have lateral softness.

- Once you have lateral flexion and softness, move your leg back, behind the back girth area, in an exaggeration of leg position 3. As you've learned, leg position 3, which

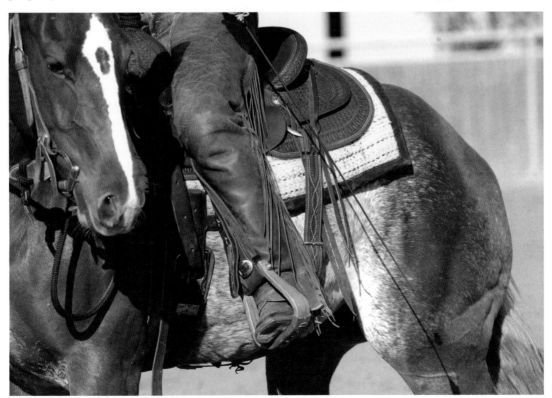

If necessary, a riding crop also can be used as reinforcement when moving the horse's hindquarters.

Practically Speaking: Applying Pressure with Leg Cues

Make sure that your stirrups are short enough to make a good bend in your leg before you apply pressure with leg cues. You must be able to move your legs easily forward and back, and in and out, but you can't if your stirrups are too long. Remember: Don't grip hard with your legs; they should rest loosely against your horse's sides unless you give your horse a cue.

Your first leg cue always should be applied with calf pressure. Turn out your toe to press your calf against your horse's side. If you must, ask two or three times with calf pressure. If your horse doesn't respond to calf pressure, lift your leg off your horse and slap his side with your leg to reinforce the cue.

Always ask your horse to yield first to your leg. If you don't get the response you want, follow through by using the end of your mecate or a riding crop. Tap with the crop or mecate in the same place you cue with your leg. If you are advanced enough in your horsemanship to ride with spurs, this is when you turn out your toe to run your rowel over your horse's side, again, in the same place you first asked with leg pressure.

Every horse has a different sensitivity level. Be as assertive as necessary to get your horse to move off your leg pressure.

moves the horse's hind end, is located along the back girth, no matter if you ride with a back girth on your saddle, or not.

- When you first teach your horse to yield to your legs, exaggerate your leg cue so that your horse understands what you want him to do. You might even need to move your leg far back, toward the horse's flank, so he really understands that you want him to move his hind end. The more advanced and refined your horsemanship becomes, the subtler your leg cue can be. But in the teaching phase you want your horse to clearly understand what pressure in each leg position means, so don't be afraid to exaggerate the cue.

- Apply leg pressure by slightly lifting your leg, turning out your toe and putting the calf against your horse's side.

- You must use a press-and-release technique with your leg. Press with your leg to apply pressure until your horse moves his hindquarters.

- Release the pressure by taking your leg off his side as soon as your horse moves. Don't maintain constant pressure; that only confuses your horse.

- Don't let go of the reins at the same time you release your leg pressure. Hold the reins until you have lateral softness, and only then give the release. Be sure to keep your hands low during this exercise.

- As you already have learned, if your horse doesn't respond to your calf pressure, rein-

force your request by lifting your leg to cue your horse more forcefully. As always, use your crop, mecate or spurs only as a last resort when working with your horse.

- As you progress with this exercise, ask your horse to move his hind end more steps each time. To supple your horse even more, ask him to yield his hindquarters around in a complete circle.

- Practice moving your horse's hindquarters in both directions, by reversing the instructions above, so that he learns to yield easily to pressure from either leg when it is in position 3.

Use Leg Position 3 to Open a Gate

I open all the ranch gates horseback because that's more efficient than dismounting, and because doing so also puts a good handle on my horse. This is a great exercise for a young horse because he sees the purpose in yielding to my leg cues.

Once you've mastered the previous leg-yielding exercise using leg position 3 to move the hindquarters, you can teach your horse to let you open a gate from the saddle. Later, you can advance to opening a gate by using the side-pass maneuver, but, for now, you can introduce the gate-opening lesson without your horse knowing how to side-pass, as described in the next chapter.

- Use leg position 3 to move your horse's hindquarters and put him into position next to the gate, close enough for you to touch it.

Opening a gate when horseback gives your horse a reason to yield to your leg cues.

Use your leg nearest the gate in position 3 to move your horse's hindquarters as you open the gate.

Practically Speaking: Put Leg-Yielding Exercises to Use

I find that horses with a lot of energy benefit greatly from the leg-yielding exercises in this chapter. That's because each exercise gives the horse a job to do. This relaxes his mind much more effectively than running him endlessly around a pen or loping him in circles for a long time.

As you work with your horse, don't drill over and over on the same exercises. Your horse becomes bored, and so do you. Work on these different leg-yielding maneuvers, but always build in progressive steps so your horse doesn't get confused. Don't move on to the next exercise until your horse has mastered each of the previous lessons.

After your horse has accomplished several exercises, mix up things to keep your riding routine from becoming dull and predictable. Don't forget: You can do these exercises on the trail or in an open field once you master them at home. Getting out of the arena goes a long way toward keeping your horse fresh, responsive and interested in his work.

To move the horse's forehand, the leg is placed in position 1 along the girth line.

- Don't fight with your horse's front end by using your reins; instead, rely on leg position 3 to move your horse where you want him to be.

- Open the gate and ride through it, using position 3 to move your horse's hindquarters around the end of the gate.

- Again, using leg position 3, move your horse back into position so you can close the gate.

- When your horse responds properly, let him stand and soak while standing near the gate.

- If your horse doesn't want to stand quietly at the gate, use leg position 3 to again move his hindquarters. Then, ask him to stand again. Let your horse rest only when he responds correctly.

Leg-Yielding the Forehand

After your horse clearly understands yielding his hindquarters when your leg is in position 3, you can teach him to yield his front end by using leg position 1. In this position, your leg is as close to the girth as possible. To be more effective, turn out your toe so your leg lies closely along the girth line.

Many of the same techniques used to move your horse's hind end apply when moving his front end.

- Remember: Constant pressure only confuses your horse. Press and release with your cueing leg to move the forehand, just as you did when moving the hind end. Be clear and emphatic with your leg cues. You want your horse to relate to your leg pressure and understand what you are asking with your cues.

- When moving your horse's forehand to the right or left with your leg in position 1, you might need to use your reins to block his forward motion. The idea is for only your horse's front end to move when your leg is in position 1, just as only his hindquarters do when your leg is position 3.

- Next, move your left leg forward into position 1 to move your horse's forehand to the right. Always first ask your horse for movement with pressure from your calf, just as you did when moving the hindquarters with your leg in position 3.

- Release your leg pressure the minute your horse responds and moves his front end, even if it's only slightly at first.

- If your horse doesn't respond to calf pressure and move his front end, follow through and ask him to move by lifting your leg off your horse and slapping his side with it, keeping your leg in position 1.

- If you still don't get the response you want, reinforce the request with the end of your mecate, riding crop or spurs. Keep in mind: These are last resorts. You don't want your horse to respond simply because he's frightened of the rein, crop or spurs.

- As you progress, you can ask your horse to move his front end more and more steps before releasing your leg cue. You even can ask him to yield his forehand around in a complete circle.

- Practice moving your horse's front end both left and right so that he learns to yield easily to pressure from either of your legs in position 1.

Two-Tracking

Two-tracking your horse is not a maneuver in itself, but rather an exercise in preparation for advanced maneuvers. Two-tracking teaches your horse to move his shoulders in response to your legs, as well as how to reach farther to cross his front feet over one other. This exercise prepares your horse for

Use a fence as a guideline when you introduce two-tracking to your horse.

When your horse responds well along the fence, move to an open area and ask him to two-track.

When your horse has mastered the two-track at a walk, increase the difficulty and pick up the pace to a trot.

After two-tracking your horse, periodically let him straighten and walk or trot on a loose rein as he relaxes.

Practically Speaking: Give Something Back

When you ride, there must be something in it for your horse. When you reward his hunger for relief, which we talked about back in Chapter 1, you give him something he understands and appreciates. Don't take away your horse's dignity. The release of pressure when he makes an effort to perform respects your horse and allows him to keep his dignity. There's nothing more fulfilling and satisfying than your horse trying his best to please you.

counter-bending, which is covered next, and actually is a step toward refining your horse's guidance and steering system because you use your legs. The less you use your reins, the more your horse can relax and use his body.

The point of this two-tracking exercise is for your horse to yield softly to your legs. When your horse two-tracks, his front feet cross over one other, but his hind feet and front feet don't travel in the same track because of a slight arc in your horse's body.

Before you can proceed with the two-tracking exercise, your horse must be soft laterally. This means that whenever you pull the rein to either side, he gives and holds his head there willingly until you release him. The more lateral flexion you have, the more respectful your horse becomes.

Lateral flexion is critical for this two-tracking exercise because your horse must start with an arc in his body—before he gives to your leg cue at position 1. However, for this exercise, your horse's nose isn't bent all the way to the side, but rather just one-quarter of the way.

• Use a fence as a guideline, riding parallel to it when you begin this exercise, which makes it easier for your horse.

• As you ride along the fence, ask your horse for lateral flexion with his head just one-quarter of the way toward the fence. With his nose to the side, his body is slightly bent opposite the direction you want to travel. If you ride with the fence at your left, your horse's head should be slightly bent to the left, or vice versa.

• Look in the direction you want to travel, right in this case.

• To travel right with your horse's head to the left, ride with your left leg in position 1, turning out your toe and pressing your calf against the horse's side, just along the girth. Although your goal is to move your horse's shoulders, don't cue your horse in front of the girth with your leg or

foot, as that causes your horse to stiffen.

• Press and release your leg in position 1 in time, or movement, with your horse's front feet. Press with your left calf when his left shoulder, closest to the fence, comes back. Release your leg pressure when that same shoulder moves forward. Don't be afraid to exaggerate your leg cue at first; you need less pressure as your horse starts to understand what you want.

• Remember: Don't leave your leg constantly against your horse, or you create resistance, which leads to a fight or causes desensitization to your leg. Follow through with firmer leg cues if your horse doesn't respond, but be sure to use the press-and-release method. This keeps your horse soft because he gets relief from pressure when he responds to your cue. To achieve softness, you always must give something back to your horse; you can't just keep taking from him without giving.

• Keep your hands low and hold your horse's head one-quarter of the way around to the left side, the entire time you are asking him to move to the right. Rest your left hand on your thigh, if necessary, so you hold your horse's nose in place without moving his head.

• There should be no pressure on the outside, right rein away from the fence; that rein should be slack. Your outside or right leg should offer no pressure; it's there only to provide support and help guide your horse through the maneuver.

• If your horse begins fighting you at any point in the two-tracking exercise, regain lateral softness before continuing and again asking your horse to two-track.

• When your horse makes an effort to two-track to the right while holding his nose to the left, release the lateral left rein to

Counter-bending your horse in a circle improves your steering as you prepare your horse for advanced maneuvers, such as the turnaround.

allow your horse to straighten his head. But always have vertical flexion, softness in his poll, before you totally release the reins and let your horse relax.

- Now let your horse relax and walk straight on a loose rein.

- You soon find that it's easier for your horse to yield to your leg when he has momentum and is moving forward.

- Reverse the above procedure to two-track your horse to the left with his nose tipped to the right as you practice two-tracking along the fence in the other direction.

Advanced Two-Tracking

When your horse understands and has mastered the two-track at a walk, you can step up your pace to a trot. It's easier to apply leg pressure at a sitting trot rather than at a posting trot. Two-tracking at a faster pace is another step forward as you progress in your training program, and mastering this exercise leads to several maneuvers, including the turnaround and rollback.

- When trotting, follow the same steps used while two-tracking at a walk. You probably will find that you don't need as much leg pressure because of your horse's more active forward movement.

- You actually "push" your horse in the trot with your leg, instead of pulling him along by your reins. The reins are there only for guidance.

- Remember: Your outside rein in the direction of travel stays slack. You want to keep that door open, not "trap" your horse with the outside rein.

- There should be an arc or bend to your horse's body the entire time you two-track and until you release his head.

- Be sure your leg stays in position 1 the entire time. If you move your leg back along your horse's side, you confuse him, and he thinks he's supposed to move his hindquarters.

- Once your horse is soft and supple at two-

tracking at both the walk and trot, you can move off the fence and try the exercise in an open area. Keep your horse on the fence until he responds well because some horses get anxious until they understand what you're asking with your leg pressure.

Counter-Bending

Master the two-track and you are ready to move on to the counter-bending exercise. This is a more advanced, exaggerated form of two-tracking because you still control the horse's shoulders, but, as he travels, his body curves around in a circle, instead of traveling straight. Counter-bending is beneficial for many advanced maneuvers, which is why I use this exercise with all my horses.

Performing a counter-bend makes the horse's rib cage supple as he yields to your leg in position 1. If your horse is stiff, his rib cage doesn't bend or give, but once he learns to supple his body in response to your leg, his entire body softens and relaxes.

"Momentum makes it easier for your horse to perform the counter-bend."

Counter-bending helps improve your steering as you prepare your horse for such maneuvers as the turnaround. You refine your steering by guiding your horse with your legs, which aids in gaining more impulsion and acceleration.

To counter-bend your horse, start with the two-track and then pick up your horse's shoulders, moving them from left to right, and vice versa. Ultimately, your horse's front leg on the same side as your cueing leg crosses over his other front leg. As your horse gains momentum, he starts to step around in a circle on the front end. He finds his rhythm and responds softly.

Once you fully accomplish the counter-bend, your horse can move in a complete circle with his body bent and with his nose turned slightly laterally in either the opposite direction his body is moving, or in his direction of travel. Again, the point of this exercise is to get your horse's body to yield easily to your leg.

When your horse responds well at the walk, advance to counter-bend him at a trot.

- Two-track your horse along the fence to your left by using the cues you've learned.

- Flex your horse's nose laterally to the left as you use your left leg in position 1, just as you did before.

- Once your horse is two-tracking well to the right, use your left leg in position 1 and put more pressure on your horse's front end until he moves to the outside, or right, and away from the fence.

- As your horse's front end moves away from the fence, release your left leg pressure. Then use the press-and-release

technique as necessary to keep your horse moving away from the fence.

- Release the left rein as soon as your horse gives to your left leg and steps across on his front end.

- Now release your rein and let your horse trot straight.

- Let your horse soak as he travels on a loose rein for a few minutes.

- Switch sides and reverse the instructions to keep your horse balanced and supple. You can perform this exercise, followed by

Real People... Real Solutions

STEPHANIE KANNAS

"Having worked under Chris, I learned how to get into the horse's mind, how to have that horse working for me instead of against me." Arlan Kannas

Raised in a ranching and rodeo family in South Dakota, Arlan Kannas has been around horses his entire life. After a career as a professional bull rider left him injured, Arlan left the rodeo arena and concentrated once again on horses. He worked as a trick rider with Dixie Stampede in Tennessee, and then became one of Monty Roberts' regular riders.

At Equine Affaire in Ohio, Arlan met Chris after watching his demonstrations. Impressed with Chris' horsemanship, Arlan moved to Texas shortly after that to work for Chris. Although already training horses, Arlan realized he could learn more and improve his skills.

"I thought Chris was an excellent horseman, above and beyond so many others," Arlan said. "Chris is a real horseman, and the proof is in the pudding. When someone can take a wild colt and in three hours have him ready to do a job, that's someone who knows how to read horses. Chris really can get into a horse's mind. He's a professional and has a Class A operation. I knew I could further my own knowledge and improve my colt-starting ability and cattle-working skills by riding with him."

Working for Chris was revolutionary, Arlan admitted. "I had some skills when I went to work for Chris, but he helped me fine-tune all those skills. He helped me sharpen my edge."

Arlan believes what he learned the most from Chris was how to sit back, read the horse and understand what he thinks. Being able to clearly read the horse showed Arlan just when to apply pressure and, even more important, when to ease the pressure.

"Having worked under Chris, I learned how to get into the horse's mind, how to have that horse working for me instead of against me," Arlan explained. "I have a lot more hindquarter control now. Taking control of the horse's hindquarters allows me to maneuver him around much better, and it makes him a lot more soft and supple. Getting control of the hind end really does give me control of the whole horse. Chris helped me to be aware of the horse's reactions, to watch for that softness and 'give' that I was looking for. I also learned how important it is to just be patient and give the horse time to soak when he's done something right.

"Chris has been really supportive now that I'm out on my own," Arlan added. "He's helped me with contacts and introduced me to people. He's not selfish and has helped me any way he can; that's the kind of man he is."

Arlan has his own training facility in Tuscaloosa, Ala., where he focuses on working ranch and reined cow horses, and schooling 2- and 3-year-olds for all-around work.

a different one, such as moving the hindquarters, and then counter-bend your horse to the other side.

- When you first introduce counter-bending, your horse curves away from the fence and moves across only a couple steps in front. Eventually, you work to counter-bend him away from the fence in a full circle.

- In the beginning stages, you want your horse's nose opposite the direction he's traveling. Once your horse has caught on to the maneuver, you can change to bend his head so that his nose goes in the same direction as his body. This gives you even more softness and control.

- After your horse responds well at the walk, you can advance to counter-bend at a trot. Momentum makes it easier for your horse to perform the counter-bend. Maintain the same press-and-release leg cue as you push your horse around the circle.

- You can ask for a tighter bend in this exercise as your horse advances, which leads to performing the turnaround.

> *"Leg position 2 moves your horse's entire body. It's easier for your horse to understand what you want if you introduce this leg position while he's in motion, instead of at a standstill."*

11

LEG-YIELDING: USING LEG POSITION 2

The more you can control your horse's body with your seat and legs, the more you can advance and refine the quality of your horsemanship. After your horse thoroughly understands what you are asking with your legs in positions 3 and 1, you can introduce leg position 2.

Before you begin leg-yielding with position 2, always review the previous lessons you've accomplished as refreshers for your horse. Make sure that you have good lateral and vertical flexion, and that you easily can move your horse's hind end with your leg in position 3 and his front end with your leg in position 1. Never move to the next step until your horse is competent with

Leg position 2 is used to move the horse's entire body when, for example, performing a side-pass.

the previous lessons you've been teaching. This is the best way to avoid "cracks" in your training foundation.

It helps greatly if you use the fence as a guideline until your horse clearly understands how to respond to your three leg positions. If your horse shows any confusion and doesn't understand what you are asking in each different position, work slowly and don't move on until he does.

Leg Position 2

Leg position 2 moves your horse's entire body. You can use leg position 2 while doing the side-pass, to move your horse from side to side when he's in motion and for flying lead changes.

This leg position is directly between position 1 along the girth line and position 3 near the hindquarters. Your horse is a good indicator to let you know when your leg is correctly

Don't advance to work with leg position 2 until your horse fully understands what you want when using your leg in positions 3 and 1.

in position 2. If your horse wants to move his hind end when you cue him with your leg in position 2, you know that your leg is too far back along his barrel. If he tries to move his front end, your leg position is too far forward. Split the difference, and you're right where you need to be for leg position 2.

Again, the angle of your leg is important; always turn out your toe so your calf is against the horse's side, just as you do when you're cueing with your leg in positions 1 or 3. Remember to use pulsating pressure, pressing and releasing your leg in time with your horse's feet, which is how you know that he's responded to your leg cue. Release your leg pressure when your horse moves his feet in the direction you want to go. Properly timing your release lets your horse know he's done the right thing, and you must give your horse that relief. As you refine your horsemanship, this pressing and releasing actually becomes just a pulsing of your leg.

Introduce the Side-Pass

Leg position 2 is essential for mastering the side-pass. You actually build on this leg position by reinforcing the desired response to your leg in positions 3 or 1. When you first begin teaching the side-pass, you must work from leg position 1 to leg position 3, and then move your leg to position 2. You find that as your horse catches on to this new cue, you can go straight to leg position 2, but in the beginning, go slowly through the previous steps so your horse clearly understands the progression. You must build the side-passing exercise a little at a time; you can't expect your horse to master this all at once. His own confidence increases as he learns he can do what you want of him.

As with the earlier leg-yielding exercises, start by working along a fence, using it to help guide your horse. It's also easier for your horse to understand what you want if you first introduce this leg position when he's moving, instead of at a standstill, because he has momentum and forward motion.

- Ride with the fence at your left and push the horse's front end to the right by using your left leg in position 1. There should be a slight arc in your horse's body as it softens to shape around your left, cueing leg although his head and neck should be straight.

When introducing the position 2 leg cue, use a fence as a guideline to help your horse understand the response you want.

- Next, use your left leg in position 3 to push your horse's hind end underneath his body and to the right. Remember to keep your toe out so your calf presses against the horse's side.

- Now move your left leg into the center position 2, to push his entire body to the right. He should begin to side-pass with both his left front and hind legs crossing over the right fore- and hind legs.

- If you aren't careful, your horse tends to bend his head, neck and shoulders in the direction you're going, so make sure to hold them straight. Don't pull on your horse's mouth or pull him into the side-pass; just hold him steady and straight.

- Look right, in the direction you're going. Use press-and-release leg cues as your horse responds to keep him moving with his front and hind legs crossing.

- Stop cueing with your leg and release the rein, but not until you have vertical softness with your horse.

- Let your horse ride on a loose rein and relax a moment.

- Reverse the previous instructions to side-pass your horse in the other direction, and practice side-passing along the fence in both directions. Since any horse tends to work better to one side, side-passing in both directions helps him progress equally on both sides.

"You can confuse and overwhelm your horse if you try to do too much at one time or do too much too soon."

Side-Pass Without the Fence

After your horse side-passes well along the fence, you can begin working without the fence as a guide. As before, in the beginning, you still need to ask your horse to yield to leg position 1. Then move your leg back to position 3 before moving to position 2. Make sure that your horse crosses his legs as he moves to the side.

In the first side-pass exercise, the fence served as the barrier, but now the reins become a barrier to keep the horse's body straight. I call it "putting a block" on the reins because I don't want to pull the horse's head to either side, but I do want to keep his neck, head and shoulders square so that his body remains straight.

When you put a block on your reins, keep them even so that your horse's neck is straight, and his head isn't turned. Don't pull back on the reins; you want only to keep him from turning to the side or from stepping forward.

Don't ask for collection, as defined in Chapter 12, when you start teaching the side-pass, but as your horse advances, you can begin to ask for more collected movement. As the horse progresses, you can, for example, bring his nose to the side and get lateral collection, with his nose facing the hip. (See Chapter 12.) This side-pass variation really develops softness in your horse's body.

- To side-pass your horse in the open, put a block on the reins to keep your horse straight and prevent his head from turning to either side, but don't pull back.

As you progress with the side-pass, rather than use the fence as a barrier, put a "block" on the reins to help position your horse.

- Work your horse in small increments at first; a few steps to the side are all you should ask for in the beginning. Always release the pressure from your leg and seat when your horse gives and moves to the side as you've asked him to do.

- Stop cueing with your leg to stop side-passing and release the rein, but only when your horse has given vertical softness.

- Ride your horse on a loose rein and let him relax before side-passing again.

- Work this side-pass exercise away from the fence in both directions.

- As your horse catches on to side-passing without the fence's aid, you can quicken the pace. You know he understands what you want when he stays soft and keeps his body straight without stiffening it.

Side-Pass From a Standstill

After you successfully master the side-pass by progressing through your leg positions while your horse is moving both on and away from the fence, you can begin to ask him to side-pass from a standstill.

Because the horse is not moving, you need to keep your reins even to help balance him. When you first ask for the side-pass from a standstill, it helps to use the fence as a guide-line. As your horse grasps what you want him to do, you then can move away from the fence to work in the open.

When side-passing, don't pull your horse sideways with the reins. Instead, think of it as "pushing" your horse into the side-pass with your leg and seat. Don't lean into the sidepass, but sit on your seat bones and push from the "outside" of your horse. If you ask your horse to side-pass to his right, for example, you press on your left seat bone—his outside—and push from this side as you press and release with your left leg. Your right leg is slightly open to allow the horse to move in this direction.

- As before, start pushing your horse's front end to the right, using your left leg in position 1. Then move your left leg back to position 3, pushing your horse's hindquarters to the right. Push with your seat and leg, but don't lean to the side. If your horse walks forward, stop and back him before continuing.

- Now move your left leg into position 2 to push your horse's entire body to the side. He should begin to side-pass, crossing both his front and hind legs.

- Look to the right, in the direction you're going. Be sure your reins are even as you block your horse with the reins, but don't pull on them.

- Use press-and-release leg pressure as your horse responds to keep him moving to the side and continuing to cross his front and hind legs. Don't look down to see if his legs cross since doing so puts your horse off balance. Instead, focus on feeling your horse's legs cross.

- Using the fence as a guide, first put a block on your reins to keep your horse's head, neck and shoulders square and aligned.

- Look right, in the direction you want to go.

Practically Speaking: Don't Make your Horse "Gate-Sour"

Some horses fixate on the gate as a way to get out of the arena and quit working. To keep a horse from becoming gate-sour, I do a variety of tasks and exercises around the gate.

When I want my horse to rest completely, I move away from the gate so he doesn't associate the gate with stopping his work. This is different from soaking, that very brief period of relaxation after accomplishing a task, which rewards the horse for a job well done.

- Turn out your left toe and press your left leg in position 2 against your horse. Press and release as you push your horse into the side-pass.

- Slightly open your opposite, or right leg, since you are moving toward the right.

- Maintain the rein block to keep your horse's body straight as he moves to the right, crossing his left front and hind legs over his right legs. If your horse turns his head to the side, he isn't properly aligned to side-pass.

- Press and release your left leg in position 2 to side-pass your horse a few steps to the right. Take your left, "pushing" leg off your horse every time he responds. Then press again to continue side-passing.

- Stop cueing with your leg and release the rein only when you've asked for and your horse has given vertical softness.

- Now ride on a loose rein and let your horse relax for a few moments.

- Practice side-passing in both directions from a standstill, reversing the cues as you travel in the opposite direction.

Side-Pass to Open Gates

You already know how to put your horse into position to open a gate by moving his hindquarters with your leg in position 3. Now fine-tune your approach and incorporate the side-pass into your gate work by using your leg in position 2. Make it a point to keep one hand on the gate at all times as you ride through the gate opening.

You can't expect to master these various side-passing exercises at one time or even in

Fine-tune your gate-opening mastery by incorporating the side-pass and leg position 2 into the maneuver, rather than using only leg positions 1 and 3.

a few lessons. Don't drill on your horse, but spice up your riding sessions and add these different exercises as your horse builds on what he knows.

- Begin with the gate to your right, for example, and your horse's head toward the gate opening. Use your left leg in position 3 to push your horse's hind end to the right and next to the gate.

- Open the gate to ride through it, keeping your right hand on the gate. Use your leg in position 3 to swing your horse's hind end around and through the gate opening.

- Now, with your horse's head toward the gate hinge, use your left leg in position 2, midway along your horse's barrel, to side-pass right close enough to the gate to shut it.

- After you have closed the gate, let your horse stand there and soak for a minute.

Leg-Yielding With Obstacles

You can continue to refine and improve your horsemanship and your horse's abilities by adding various leg-yielding exercises to your routine, as long as the exercises progressively build on what your horse already has learned. This increases his confidence and keeps him from getting bored.

It's better to build skills a little bit every time you ride your horse, rather than to introduce too much at once. You can confuse and over-

Before schooling your horse on the side-pass, first introduce him to the pole obstacle you plan to use.

Using two poles as an "L" obstacle increases the degree of difficulty as you and your horse work to hone your skills.

When your horse's hindquarters are within the L, you must maneuver his forehand around the corner before again side-passing to the end of the pole.

129

whelm your horse if you try to do too much at one time or do too much too soon. As always, end your riding session by doing a maneuver your horse is comfortable with and knows.

After your horse thoroughly understands what you ask of him with your leg in position 2 and can side-pass in both directions, you can make things more interesting by introducing an obstacle.

I like the following "L" exercise because it allows me to use all three leg positions on the horse as he negotiates the obstacle. But first I must introduce my horse to a pole. Here's how to do that.

Change your routine by asking your horse to side-pass through the obstacle with his hindquarters outside the L.

In this situation, you must maneuver your horse's hindquarters around the corner before resuming the side-pass.

Practically Speaking: Sit and Soak

Always give your horse the chance to relax and soak after he accomplishes an exercise. The more advanced your horsemanship, the more valuable your horse's soaking periods become. Reinforce the positive by rewarding him with soaking periods throughout your training sessions.

Think of your horse as a sponge. A damp sponge is soft and can absorb, while a dry sponge is hard and nonabsorbent. The same principle applies to your horse: If he's soft and responsive, he absorbs the lesson, but when he's stiff and resistant, he doesn't learn.

Never underestimate the benefit of sitting quietly and giving your horse a few moments to absorb the lesson he's just learned.

Practically Speaking: Body-Reining

I like to think of "body-reining" as a more accurate way to describe neck-reining because, when it's done right, the horse's entire body should be involved.

If you practice body-reining, you can enhance the finished turnaround. Here are some pointers for body-reining your horse.

- Your rein hand should be flat as you direct your horse's nose in the direction you want to go. Don't twist your wrist as you guide your horse.

- Don't lean to the inside of the turn, but press with your outside leg, the leg opposite the direction you are reining your horse.

- Keep your weight on your seat bone that's to the outside of your turn.

- Direct your horse through the turn and then put your hand back in neutral position.

- Let your horse walk smoothly out of the turn.

- First, lay a single pole flat on the ground. Allow your horse to investigate it, dropping his head, if he wants, to sniff the pole.

- Using your leg in position 2, ask your horse to side-pass over the pole in one direction. Then stop him and side-pass him over the pole in the opposite direction.

Once your horse has mastered the previous task, you can add a second pole so that the two ground poles are in an "L" shape. This exercise is great for using all three leg positions.

- Start, for example, with your horse at the upper end of the L, the pole to your right and your horse's head inside the L.

- Side-pass from left to right along the pole until you get to the corner of the L.

- At the corner, move your left leg to position 3 to push your horse's hind end from left to right around the corner while his front feet stay in place.

- Now side-pass right to the end of the second pole.

- Reverse the instructions to side-pass over the poles again, this time in the opposite direction. With your horse's head still inside the L, side-pass from right to left.

- Next, reverse your approach to the L, positioning your horse's hindquarters inside the L, and side-pass from right to left the length of the upper end of the L. This time you must move your horse's forehand around the corner to continue side-passing over the second pole.

Perfect the Turnaround

As your horse becomes softer and more responsive to your legs, you can build on leg-yielding exercises you learned in the previous chapter. For example, the turnaround really is just a progression of the counter-bending exercise you've already accomplished. Performing a turnaround is an excellent way to stay out of your horse's mouth yet, at the same time, increase control of his body.

For your horse to master the turnaround, he must move off your leg pressure. If for any reason he doesn't give to your leg pressure, go back to work on the counter-bending exercises until your horse is more responsive. Before polishing the turnaround, your horse should move quickly away from your leg pressure and counter-bend easily away from the fence in a full circle.

In the beginning of the previous counter-bend work you had your horse's head bent to the outside of the circle, but as he advances, you turn his head so that his nose points in the same direction his body goes. When that happens, as you begin to tighten the circle, you move toward perfecting the turnaround.

At first, it helps to get as close as you can to the fence, so you can use it to help with the turnaround; doing so encourages your horse to turn away when you cue him with your leg in position 1. First trot alongside the fence and then turn into it, so the fence serves as a block to help lift, or elevate, your horse's front end. Instead of turning all the way around in a 360-degree circle, start by turning into the fence and doing a rollback of 180 degrees to one side. You gain momentum as you teach your horse to do a rollback off the fence.

The difference between a rollback and a turnaround: When doing a rollback, the horse elevates his front end and puts his weight on his hindquarters. He picks up his front feet and brings them through the air, as opposed to the turnaround, when he steps his feet over and across one another. To achieve a rollback, I back a horse a little more on his hind end to put more weight there. Then I use my outside leg to pick up the front end as I bring the horse's nose around in a 180-degree turn.

As you progress, instead of letting your horse roll back only 180 degrees, keep him stepping around with his forehand and then let him trot out of the maneuver. Eventually, your horse steps around in a complete circle, performing a 360-degree turnaround. Here's how to reach that point with your horse.

- With the fence on your left, ride as close to it as possible and still allow room for your horse to turn into the fence.

- Hold the reins in both hands and maintain a bridge between your hands. Always keep your hands forward as you bring your horse's front end around through the turn into the fence.

- Now, with your left leg in position 1, turn your horse's front end right and away from the fence. Stay to the "outside" of the turn, and use just enough left leg pressure to get your horse to move through the turn.

Before working on 360-degree turnarounds, work closely to the fence as you stop your horse and roll him into the fence to reverse his direction.

As you first trot and then later canter your horse, use the fence as a block to help your horse perform a 180-degree rollback.

Your horse's nose leads the way as his body follows through the turn along the fence.

As your horse completes the rollback along the fence, he is positioned for a canter departure on the correct lead.

When your horse understands how to perform a rollback against the fence, ask him to perform the maneuver in the open.

- Ride from the "outside in" and release your leg pressure as your horse's front end moves right and away from the fence. Continue to press and release your left leg to keep your horse moving right, into and then away from the fence as he travels around in a full circle.

- To maintain your horse's forward momentum, press with your outside leg so that he steps across and then trots out of the circle at the end of the turnaround. Your outside leg is what speeds up and collects your horse into the turn.

- As you ask your horse to quit turning and leave the circle, release your leg pressure totally as he straightens to move forward.

- Release the lateral right rein, and then ask for and get vertical softness before you totally release the reins. Always make sure your horse is soft vertically before you release the rein after a turnaround.

- Let your horse soak as you ride with a loose rein for a few minutes.

- Practice turning into and away from the

In previous counter-bend work, the horse's nose was tipped outside the circle, in this case, to the right.

Now I begin to straighten my horse's neck and bring his head around as I turn.

Here, my horse's nose begins to lead the way through the left-hand turnaround.

As I refine my horse's skills, he turns around easily and with slack in the reins.

Don't roll your hand on the reins and bring up your thumb as you turn your horse.

Don't ride with uneven reins because doing that confuses and misdirects your horse.

Do keep your knuckles up when your reins are crossed and you ask your horse to turn.

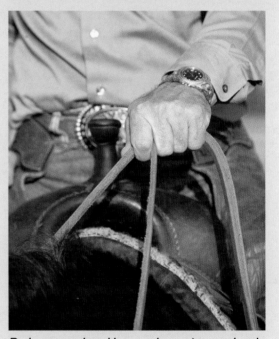

Do keep your knuckles up when using one hand and a finger between your reins to turn.

fence in both directions, so your horse learns to turn 360 degrees to both the left and the right.

- Now ride down the fence—without turning at times. Don't turn your horse every time, or he soon anticipates the turn.

- Don't be concerned about perfecting the turnaround in one or two sessions. That won't happen. This is a building exercise, and you need to have the building blocks—the previous lessons—in place before you get to this point of fine-tuning and perfecting the turnaround.

Real People...Real Solutions

CAROL MINGST.

"With effective leg-yielding, I find that everything about your riding improves."
Susan Dockter

Having ridden her entire life, Susan Dockter of Danville, Calif., became seriously committed to developing her horsemanship skills in the early 1990s. She studied under several prominent natural horsemanship clinicians before meeting Chris at a four-day Horsemanship I clinic he was teaching in California in 2006. Susan had brought her horse and signed up to ride in the clinic when she learned space was available. That serendipitous action would change the direction of her riding career.

"I had met a lot of clinicians and was disappointed because I knew what they were teaching couldn't be getting the results they were showing," said Susan. "I didn't believe in any of them anymore. Unfortunately, a lot of people out there don't use the same methods in private that they use in public. What Chris does when he's training a horse at home is exactly the same as how he works with a horse in a demonstration or at an expo. There's nothing he does differently 'behind the scenes.'"

Already an accomplished horsewoman, Susan, who presently rides an Arabian and a National Show Horse, has a bevy of North American Trail Ride Conference awards from her days in competitive trail riding. Currently active in dressage and jumping, Susan works as a horse trainer, as well as a riding instructor, having left her former position as a national account manager for a large payroll company in corporate America to pursue her dreams of working with horses professionally.

After participating in that first clinic with Chris, she admitted she was "blown away by him. We saw eye to eye on a lot of things. After that clinic, he invited me to come to Texas to study with him," she recalled. "I went and took Horsemanship II and III back to back. Then a few months later, I returned and took Horsemanship IV. His methods cross all disciplines. Working with him really cleaned up what I was doing. One of the most important things I learned from Chris is that it's not about desensitization, it's about respect."

Because she regularly teaches trail clinics, Susan often works with riders who have trouble getting their horses to respond to leg cues. Susan shows them how to use leg-yielding exercises to develop and refine their leg aids. These exercises are especially helpful on the trail, where riders always are negotiating obstacles. Teaching a horse to respond to his rider's leg is very helpful when a sensitive horse becomes anxious or evasive the more the reins are used.

"With effective leg-yielding, I find everything about your riding improves," Susan said. "If you can position your horse exactly where you want him, then you see how effective your legs really are. A lot of people think they're using their legs, but they actually are using their reins much more than they are aware. Most people correct their horses with their reins if they don't immediately get results with their leg cues. One thing that makes Chris different is that he does the majority of correction with his legs."

The emphasis on leg-yielding and proper use of the rider's legs in Chris' program helps Susan on a daily basis as she works with students and their horses.

"When a horse is truly collected, this collection is evident throughout his entire body, not just in his head position. ... Collection starts from the hindquarters and works forward."

12

COWBOYS AND COLLECTION

Mention the word "collection," and people often have different images. Some picture a dressage horse performing a powerful extended trot with his head held perfectly vertical and his hind end driving him forward. Others might think of a racehorse warming up, tight as a coiled spring and fighting the bit, head tucked into his chest.

When a horse is truly collected, this collection is evident throughout his entire body, not just in his head position. Actually, the head is the last piece to fall into place. Collection starts from the hindquarters and works forward. A collected horse powers himself forward with his hind end driving deeply beneath his body. When you think about it, just about

Collection starts from the horse's hindquarters and works forward, no matter the gait.

139

When a horse's head is overbent and behind the vertical, he can't achieve collection.

Flexed correctly at the poll, a horse can achieve collection in any maneuver.

everything we do with the horse—if we do it correctly—starts from the hind end and moves forward.

You want your horse to be soft and balanced, but if his chin drops too close to his chest, he's overbent, behind the vertical, and he can't achieve collection this way. An inexperienced rider might think a horse is collected when his head is tucked like that, but with the horse's nose overbent, more weight transfers to the horse's front end instead of to his hind end. The only way a horse can be collected is when driving those hindquarters deeply beneath his body.

The other extreme is the horse whose head carriage is far above the vertical. This type of head carriage hollows the horse's back, and he travels in a strung-out fashion without using his hind end properly.

When your horse is collected, you have vertical flexion as he breaks at the poll with his nose down. His hind end is underneath him so that his hind legs can reach beneath his body to drive him forward, and his back is rounded, or arched. With true refined collection, the horse is soft—not resisting your hands in any way.

As you begin teaching your horse collection, you must realize that this cannot be achieved in a day or a week. You can't expect a young or inexperienced horse to maintain collection for more than short periods at the time. You need to build from seconds of collection to minutes of collection, and the horse needs frequent short breaks during each lesson. You have to build gradually, so that he's able to hold collection for any length of time.

The goal is for your horse to respond, or give, both physically and mentally. As with all the other lessons, there must be relief for the horse. If not, his body might give, but his mind doesn't, and you end up with a frustrated, resentful horse.

Get Started

Before you ever try to collect your horse, make sure he responds softly and gives to you both laterally and vertically with ease. The longer your horse stays soft in vertical flexion, the longer you can keep him collected. Check your throatlatch and be certain it isn't too snug, which can interfere with vertical flexion and be uncomfortable for your horse.

Your leg, seat and hand positions drive your horse to collection, so you want to master these positions first at a standstill, and then move your horse into a walk. To be collected, your horse needs impulsion and must move forward, but you should feel confident about your position before asking him to move.

Position yourself to achieve collection by holding your reins with both hands, with a bridge between them so that your hands stay even. Ride in the center seat position, position 2. You use your arms to form a brace with your reins, but this doesn't mean you pull back on your reins. You just hold them in the position where you want your horse to find collection. In other words, if your horse carries his head too high or too low, he encounters pressure on the reins. He soon learns to put his head in a certain position, where there is no pressure when you pick up the reins. It doesn't take long for him to find that collected, vertical "sweet spot."

In the beginning, as soon as your horse finds the desired head carriage, give him a release with your reins. As he learns collection, you can hold him there in position for longer periods of time.

To achieve collection, a horse must be able to flex vertically and laterally, and the rider must effectively use his hand, seat and leg positions.

Use a bridge in your reins and keep your reins even to help your horse find that collected, vertical "sweet spot."

Collection at a Walk

Once you have consistent lateral and vertical flexion and are confident about your body position, you can ask your horse for collection at the walk. As you work to collect your horse's frame, always give him plenty of breaks, and don't ask him to hold collection for more than a few seconds in the beginning. He gets tired and resentful if you force him to hold collection very long, especially at first. Collection isn't easy for a horse until he understands what you are asking of him and becomes more physically fit to hold this position.

When you initially introduce collection, don't ask your horse to maintain his collected walk for too long without giving him a break.

- First, ask your horse for vertical flexion. Keep a bridge in your reins, form a brace with your arms, and keep your arms straight and forward.

- Riding in the center position 2, drive the horse forward by squeezing with both your lower legs.

- Continue to hold the rein brace, but don't pull back on the reins.

- If your horse fights or pushes against the bit, maintain the brace, and ride more assertively with your legs to drive your horse forward into collection.

- When your horse moves forward and becomes soft in the vertical head position you want, release your hold.

- Remember that your horse learns when you give him the relief he needs. Provide release when your horse responds prop-

erly and gives to you, and he soon seeks the proper response because he understands that this is his reward.

"I want the horse collected mentally, as well as physically."

Collection at a Trot

You can work on collecting your horse at a trot after you have the basics down at the walk. For a collected trot, use the same cues that you do at the walk. Rather than starting to achieve collection at a posting trot, work first at a sitting trot. At the sitting trot, it's easier to drive your horse forward with your legs since you aren't rising and falling in the saddle as you post.

As you practice riding with collection, be sure to ride in both directions and in circles since some horses can be more resistant on one side than the other. This is common,

Collection work doesn't have to be confined to the arena. You can collect your horse anytime and anywhere you ride.

and the only way you can overcome that resistance is by practicing maneuvers to even up your horse's sides.

After your horse has learned how to collect himself in an enclosed area, start asking for short periods of collection when riding on the trail. You also can incorporate some of the previous exercises you've learned, such as two-tracking, counter-bending, side-passing or turnarounds, and perform them with collection. The variety keeps things interesting for both you and your horse.

Collection at a Canter

The horse's body position is very different at the canter than it is at the trot, so it's important that you master collection at the walk and trot before speeding up things. Remember that your hand and leg positions are critical for communicating the cues for collection.

Before attempting collection at the canter, make sure your horse gives vertically at the poll at both a walk and trot. He must be soft, responsive and giving to you at these slower gaits before you ask him to canter.

When collected at the canter, your horse travels higher in front because his back is slightly rounded. His hind end seems lower because his hind legs drive deeply beneath his body. His gathered frame becomes soft, not stiff and resistant. Your horse can't round his back to get his hindquarters underneath him when he's stiff.

- Gain vertical flexion and remind the horse to give as you create a brace with your hands and arms.

- Drive your horse forward using your lower legs. Ride in the center seat position 2 and squeeze evenly with both legs. Your legs, not your hands or the rein pressure, encourage your horse to give and soften.

- Continue to drive your horse forward with your legs and seat, and canter until he relaxes.

- When your horse canters forward with his head softly positioned on the vertical, give back to him. Don't maintain pressure without giving him that release. Always give back immediately when your horse softens and responds to pressure.

- Work your horse in both directions while you maintain vertical flexion and softness.

Add Refinement to Collection

My goal is always to achieve collection with softness. I want the horse collected mentally, as well as physically. There is nothing attractive about a collected horse that fights it with every stride. I want to be able to drive my horse forward with my seat and legs at all three gaits—walk, trot and canter—without any resistance, and to have him on a soft rein.

You should always look for and encourage that softness. Every time you stop, never let the reins go until your horse is soft and giving.

There are several things you can do to refine your collection:

- Soften your horse's response by asking him to give his nose to the left and to the right while he's collected.

- Ride small, tight circles if you need to gain control of your horse.

- Expand to ride larger circles as your horse relaxes in his work.

- Focus on controlling your horse, yet encouraging collection with your seat and legs—not with your hands. I can't say enough about holding the brace, but without pulling on the horse's mouth.

- Make it a point to feel the collection without looking down at your horse to see if he's collected. If he is, you can feel it.

- Pick a point and ride your horse toward it. Your focus always should be up and looking forward in the direction you want to go

Pick Your Point and Ride

Use this exercise frequently to refine collection and to enhance control of your horse.

When collected at the canter, your horse's back is slightly rounded, his hind legs drive deeply beneath his body, and his head is on the vertical.

This also drives home to you, as a rider, the importance of focusing in the direction you want to go and how much your horse picks up on this. As you look where you want to go, focus on having your energy flow through your body and into your horse.

Practically Speaking: Handle the Reins for Collection

When I pick up my reins and put a brace on them to teach collection, I move slowly in the beginning. But later I build on this so the horse accepts me moving at different speeds.

A lot of people move cautiously and gather up their reins in slow motion, thinking they'll scare their horses. I want my horse to feel comfortable with me moving at different speeds. I want him to accept my hands moving fast and at all different heights, so that when pressure is applied, he quickly finds that collected, vertical soft spot. I want it to become a habit for the horse to put his head in that position as soon as I pick up my reins to ask for vertical softness.

Let your horse relax in his work by loping a few minutes before you ask for collection again.

You don't have to do this exercise with your horse collected every time, but he always should be balanced and smoothly moving in the direction you've asked and at the speed you've chosen.

This is a great exercise to do in a field or an arena. The idea is to pick a "target," whatever you decide—a post, tree, shadow or sign—and ride straight toward it. Visually remain focused on your target the entire time, even if your horse veers off course. Ideally, once you set your horse on a straight path, he should continue until you reach the target. But you might be surprised how much steering and guiding some horses need. This is a good test to discover how much refinement you have developed and how much in harmony you are with your horse.

Don't tell your horse to move before telling him which direction to go. Cue your horse in this order when guiding or steering him: 1) direct rein, 2) indirect rein and 3) leg pressure. If you cue him first with your leg and he moves, but not in the direction you want, you must correct him immediately. So first pick up the reins and direct your horse.

Then use your reins and legs to keep your horse's nose and body in line with where you are headed. You need to guide your horse only if he starts to veer away from this direction. If he does, block his movement with your reins and legs as necessary. Pressure from both your legs tells your horse to accelerate in the direction you're headed. Pressure from one leg or the other is used to steer or guide him. As soon as your horse turns in the direction you want, immediately take your leg off him. This way he understands that pressure from one leg does not mean to increase his speed.

The goal is for your horse to go in the direction you select and continue that way until and unless you cue him otherwise. He should travel at the pace you select, without speeding up or slowing down until you ask him to do so. When he travels straight in the correct direction, relax and ride. Both your seat and legs should be in position 2, and there should be no pressure from either your legs or the reins when your horse travels evenly and straight to the target.

Here's how to get your horse on target.

- Pick a target and visually focus on it throughout the exercise.

- With your reins, first direct your horse toward the target.

- After guiding your horse with the reins, cue him with leg pressure to move forward.

- Use your reins and legs to keep your horse's nose and body straight in the direction you're headed and to maintain his forward motion.

- Steer or guide your horse only if he veers off course. Block him with your reins and legs as needed for correction.

- Keep your legs loose and relaxed unless you need to guide your horse. When you

As my horse relaxes for a moment, I select the next point toward which we'll ride when I again ask him to travel in a collected manner.

Tip your horse's nose and ask him to back in a circle in the same direction to hone your "collective" skills.

do use your legs, release the pressure as soon as your horse goes in the direction you ask

.

- Practice this exercise first at a walk and then a trot, before moving to a canter. If your horse isn't soft and responsive to your leg movements, go back to the counter-bending and two-tracking exercises. Exaggerate your cues until your horse yields to the pressure and responds correctly.

Lateral Collection

Your horse already is well-versed in giving to the side when you ask for lateral flexion, but you also can add collection in maneuvers by asking your horse to give laterally and tuck his nose at the same time. The following exercise is great practice for refining your rollbacks and turnarounds.

- Ask for lateral flexion. Bring your horse's nose to the side as you've learned to do.

Practically Speaking: Spice Things Up!

There are so many different things we can do with horses, and I admire any of those that give a horse purpose. We might enjoy schooling exercises as we seek to improve and better our horsemanship skills, but we must remember that, the way the horse sees things, arena maneuvers don't really have purpose.

This is why I like to add variety to my riding routine and spice up things for the horse. I might add low jumps for a dressage horse, or take a show horse out of the arena and down the trail. I also like to take a horse out in the pasture to move cattle. Even though a horse has never even been around cattle, once he gets used to them, the horse enjoys the job of making the cattle move from here to there. The horse can see the reason behind what is being asked of him, and he appreciates this. I often have course students move cattle, and they are amazed at how much the horses get into this job once they get the hang of it.

Giving the horse a task to accomplish builds his confidence. Never underestimate how much you can teach the horse when you aren't drilling him on exercises and maneuvers.

- If, for example, your horse's nose is tipped to the left, pick up the outside or opposite right rein, just as you would to ask for vertical flexion. This causes your horse to flex at the poll and tuck his nose although his head is still tipped laterally to the side.

- Don't ask for anything else until your horse is laterally collected and soft throughout his body.

- When your horse becomes soft and collected, ask him to back in a circle and in the same direction that his nose is tipped in this case, to the left.

- Your horse should arc backward around the circle, moving off your legs as you guide him with your reins.

- After backing your horse in a complete circle, make sure you have soft lateral flexion and then release your horse.

- Back your horse in the circle in both directions.

"The horse picks up and changes leads in the hind end first, so concentrating on his front end can be deceiving."

13
LEADS AND CHANGES SIMPLIFIED

Call it a "canter" or a "lope." By either name this gait is a challenge for many riders, but it doesn't have to be that way. Even more confusing, the horse should canter or lope in the correct lead, which can be the right or left one, depending on his path of travel, and he can change that lead when he changes direction.

When a horse canters, one front leg reaches ahead more than the other, just as the hind leg on the same, leading side of the horse's body reaches ahead of the other hind leg. When the left front and rear legs extend most, the horse is on the left lead; when the right legs reach farther, he's on the right lead. Anytime

When traveling in a circle to the right, the horse's inside, or right, foreleg and hind leg seem to lead the action, with the outside legs trailing slightly behind.

151

Place your hand on your horse's hindquarters to feel when each hind foot lands.

you canter in a circle, you ask the horse to pick up whichever lead is to the inside of the circle. That is considered the "correct" lead. For example, when cantering in a circle to the left, you want your horse on his left lead; when cantering to the right, your horse should be on his right lead.

For the horse, picking up either the right or left lead, or even changing leads in mid-stride, is no big deal. It's totally natural for him. Watch a group of horses at play in the pasture and you're bound to see numerous flying changes of lead performed smoothly and easily. The problem comes when a rider enters the picture and tries to control just when those changes are made. We take something that is second nature to the horse and

complicate it by asking him to perform in the wrong way or at the wrong time.

Many riders mistakenly concentrate on the horse's front end when asking the horse to canter or to change leads. The truth of the matter: The horse picks up and changes leads in the hind end first, so concentrating on his front end can be deceiving. The horse might "cross-fire," or be on one lead on the front end, but on the opposite lead behind. He even can pick up the lead you want in front, but be on the wrong lead behind.

Once again, your focus needs to be on the hind end in order to avoid lead and lead-changing problems. If you get your horse to take the correct lead behind, he can pick up or change to the correct lead in front. The correct lead departure actually starts as you move your horse's hind end in the direction of the lead you want him to take.

When the horse is on the right lead, his right hind leg should come slightly farther beneath his body than his left hind. His right front leg also should reach farther than his left front. The exact opposite is true when the horse is on the left lead.

As you've learned, so much happens with a horse's hind end. All you should do with the front end is keep your horse's body straight and support him so that he doesn't drop a shoulder and get off balance. It's actually easy to change leads on a horse, even one that has not been ridden much, if you can relax him and put him into position to change the weight distribution on his inside and outside hind legs. Then he's able to pick up either lead when you ask him.

In Sync with the Footfall

Before you can successfully and consistently take a lead or change leads on your horse, you must understand where his feet are at all times. You might think, "Well, that's easy. His feet are underneath him!" True, but there's a lot more to it than that. I put a lot of emphasis on knowing exactly where my horse's feet are and how they land.

You, too, must know where your horse's feet are and how they naturally fall when he canters in order to perform lead departures and changes correctly. This applies whether you ride English or Western.

The key to mastering leads is getting in rhythm with your horse's movement, so you can tune in to his footfall. Your horsemanship, timing and feel improve dramatically once you really learn to get in sync with that natural rhythm. So many people want to look for the horse's rhythm, but I always tell my students, "Looking is cheating." You can't see "feel;" you must develop it.

To start familiarizing yourself with your horse's footfall, first ride at a walk. Place one hand behind the saddle and on your horse's hindquarters so you can feel his hind feet as they land. Once you can feel that landing with your hand, concentrate on feeling that rhythm coming through the horse's hindquarter muscles and into your seat. Look in the direction you're going; don't look down to see exactly where your horse's feet are.

Now pick up a posting trot on the correct diagonal and focus on feeling where your horse's feet land. Feel that rhythmic motion as his diagonal legs move together, and be especially aware of each hind leg coming underneath his body and then landing as he travels. You can do this any time you ride, and I encourage you to practice this as often as necessary until knowing your horse's footfall becomes automatic.

Lead Departures

If you want to make a lead departure as simple as possible, preparation is important. Your horse should be supple and give easily to you in both directions. You rely on the groundwork you've built through the earlier exercises, and your horse should understand clearly how to do them.

Your horse should be able to pivot off his front end in either direction. Because the hind end is where the lead departure and the lead change begin, being able to move your horse's hindquarters is critical. If you

For a canter departure to the right, use your left leg to push your horse's hindquarters to the right.

The right leg is used to cue your horse for a left lead canter departure.

Practically Speaking: Make Warm-Up Work for You

Riders often ask if they really need a designated warm-up period before they begin working their horses. Although I've found that horses vary in how much time each needs to really focus and get down to business, every horse benefits physically from a short warm-up session. It not only loosens and warms his muscles, but also settles his mind and helps him concentrate on his rider and the work at hand.

I like to begin a warm-up period with a short session of groundwork, using only a halter and lead rope. This very quickly lets me know my horse's frame of mind. Then I saddle and do simple riding exercises, such as leg-yielding, so my horse has a chance to loosen up. I always change directions several times as I warm up a horse and check his responsiveness.

Some riders go directly into a canter and use this gait as a warm-up, but I don't recommend that. I always start at a walk and trot before moving on to the canter.

When a horse feels fresh and wants to canter before I ask him, I use one of two methods of correction, depending on his personality. If the horse just feels eager, I most likely use a direct correction and bring him back to the gait I requested.

But when a horse really challenges or tries to resist me, I often go with reverse psychology. In this case, he wants to canter, so I let him do just that, but I keep him cantering longer than he wants. I also change his direction frequently, for example, by having him roll back along the fence. I keep him going until I ask him to stop—not just until he feels like stopping.

I often use this reverse psychology with horses. Going against the horse's strength isn't a wise move; he always is stronger and can overpower you. You must use your mind and skills instead of relying on brute force to achieve your goals.

As always, there's a difference between teaching a horse and correcting him. When a horse does something wrong because he doesn't know, then you show him the right way by teaching him. When the horse does something even though he knows it's wrong, you need to correct him. You basically use the same cues for both teaching and correcting, but your application with the disobedient horse has more energy; your asking has more escalation because you are correcting, not teaching.

---

can easily move his hind end, you can put your horse into position to pick up the correct lead. The leg-yielding exercises you have learned come into play here.

Riding at a slow walk and using leg position 2, practice pushing your horse's hind end from side to side. At this point, your horse shouldn't need the exaggeration of you putting your leg into position 3 to move his hind end, but you can use this position if you need to remind him of the desired response. Positioning the hindquarters is the secret to picking up the correct lead in a canter departure. Your horse's weight must be on his inside hind leg as he moves into the lead departure in a given direction, for example, on his right hind leg as he canters on the right lead in that direction, or vice versa.

Use your "outside" leg and seat to move your horse into the correct position for a lead departure. When I refer to the outside leg, this means your leg on the outside of the circle you ride. The "inside" leg is your leg inside the circle. Your outside leg pushes your horse's hindquarters, so that his inside hind leg picks up the correct lead. You always use your outside leg more than your inside leg when asking for a lead departure.

If you want to pick up the right lead, for example, your outside, left leg pushes your horse's hindquarters to the right, so that his right hind leg picks up the correct lead. To pick up the left lead, your right leg becomes the outside leg, pushing your horse's hindquarters left so that his left hind leg picks up the left lead.

"If we learn to ask the horse correctly and stay out of his way, the process becomes simple."

Here's how to ask your horse for a canter departure on a specific lead, in this case, the left lead.

- Ride at a walk and keep your eyes forward and focused in the direction you want to go.

- Ride centered in seat position 2 with your weight on your outside or right seat bone to help "push" your horse into the desired left lead.

- Keep your horse's head straight. Don't pull his head left, to the inside, to pick up the left lead because doing so only pushes your horse's hind end to the outside, or right, and off-lead.

- Move into a trot and push with your outside right leg in position 2 until your horse moves his inside left hind leg to canter. His weight must be on the inside hind leg for him to pick up the correct, in this case, left lead. Again, your horse shouldn't need an exaggerated leg cue in position 3. If he does, work on the previous side-pass exercises to sharpen your horse's response to your leg in position 2.

- Keep your horse's head and body straight after he is cantering in the correct lead.

- Reverse the directions for a canter departure in the right lead. Practice making lead departures in each direction, as horses often favor one side, or lead, over the other, but don't focus on one side, even though your horse's response might seem worse in that direction.

- When asked for a lead departure, a young or inexperienced horse often canters faster than you want. If this happens, don't pull your horse down to a trot. Instead, continue cantering, but travel in smaller circles until your horse slows and "comes back" to you. Again, practice picking up both leads.

- After your horse has learned to move from a trot into a canter, begin refining your canter departure until your horse can move immediately into the canter from a walk or even a standstill. To accomplish this, you must hold a brace with the reins to block your horse from walking or trotting forward, while giving your horse slight slack in the rein on the side of the desired lead. For example, to take the right lead, hold your horse's head straight, but offer slightly more slack in the right rein. Then use your left, outside leg to push your horse's hindquarters to the right. To pick up the left lead, use the left rein and your outside, right leg to push the horse's hind quarters to the left.

The Flying Change

It's a piece of cake for your horse to change leads any time he feels like it. Flying

My horse canters on his left lead as we approach the point where we'll change to the right lead.

changes of lead are totally natural maneuvers for him. We muddy the waters by getting in his way and by not asking the horse properly to change leads. If we learn to ask the horse correctly and stay out of his way, the process becomes simple.

When you run into a lead-changing problem, it's usually a sign that your horse's performance isn't solid on the exercises described in the earlier chapters. First, go back and refine your work on these exercises before you proceed to lead changes. Your horse must be absolutely clear on all three leg-cue positions and give to your leg pressure at all gaits before you can advance to change leads at the canter. For example, you should be able to move your horse's hind end using leg position 2 at this point. If you must put your leg completely back and into position 3, work on the previous side-pass exercises to sharpen your horse's response to your leg in position 2.

Always work on lead departures first, as a building block before you advance and ask your horse to change leads.

Remember: Don't pull your horse's head into the change. Your horse must be balanced

My horse is mid-change, about to take his right lead and move into a right circle.

With his right hind engaged, his right leading leg will strike the ground ahead of his left front foot.

My horse's left hind is just about to engage as he changes leads to travel to the left.

My horse is again cantering on his left lead.

The more comfortable you are loping your horse and the smoother your canter departures, the easier it becomes to master lead changes.

to change leads; you help him stay balanced by not leaning in the saddle or pulling on his head. Instead, use your body to push his body, so that he switches leads; think of it as a "mini side-pass" in motion.

I can't stress this enough: You cannot expect immediate results when you first put your leg on your horse for a lead change. He won't respond right away. You must be patient and wait on the change.

In the beginning, asking for a lead change while going over an obstacle, such as a pole on the ground, can help your horse transfer his weight as he changes leads. But you must be sure to keep his body straight as he goes over the pole. You don't want him to travel crooked.

Here's how to ride your horse through a lead change.

- Ride at a slow canter with your horse in the left lead. Use your left leg in position 2 to gently push your horse into a side-pass to the right, the direction of the lead you want him to take. When your horse lopes on the left lead and you want him to change to the right lead, your left leg should push his hind end to the right, or vice versa when changing from the right to the left lead.

- Look in the direction you want to go, for example, to the right, and keep your shoulders square with your horse's shoulders.

- When changing from the left to the right lead, take your weight off your right seat bone and push it onto your left seat bone, but don't lean into the change.

Real People... Real Solutions

DUTCH NICHOLS

"Chris is the first person to ever emphasize to me how important it is to feel the footfall. ... This knowledge and feel carries over into so many areas." Katie Nichols

"I had not ridden until my husband bought me my first horse when I was 27," said Katie Nichols, a Templeton, Calif., bookkeeper and horse owner. "After I met Chris, I realized I wasn't really riding. I was just sitting on the horse's back, but I happened to have some incredible horses that were so well broke, I had no problems."

After seeing Chris perform a demonstration at Equine Experience in Paso Robles, Calif., Katie realized how much she still needed to learn. She'd just purchased a new horse, one far more refined and athletic than any horse she'd owned previously. At that same expo she signed up her husband and herself for Chris' Horsemanship I and Horsemanship II courses.

"With my new horse, Trumby, I realized I didn't have the tools I needed to really ride," Katie said. "He's an amazing horse and far more advanced than I was. I found I was doing too much at one time and was 'overcommunicating' to him. I was making things more complicated than they needed to be. I think this is a common problem for many riders. The horse is listening to all the rider's body movements and gets confused. Communication between horse and rider should be simple, and if you can just be still on the horse and ask him in the right way, it becomes clear to the horse."

As do many riders, Katie found that she too often relied on sight instead of feel. This was especially obvious when it came to leads and lead changes.

"Things finally came together for me when I realized that feeling the horse's footfall was the beginning preparation for picking up the correct lead," she noted. "Chris is the first person to ever emphasize to me how important it is to feel the footfall. I really had to concentrate on this. I understood that feeling the footfall was the key that I was missing.

"Whenever I was on the horse's back, I made it a point to concentrate on feeling where his feet were. It takes a little while to get it, but once you do, you have it. And now that I do, I'm thrilled! This knowledge and feel carries over into so many areas. For example, now when I stop my horse, I know to ask him to prepare to stop when his hind feet are in the right position so he can stop correctly.

"Chris changed the way I ride by giving me the knowledge and techniques I needed," Katie added. "I've been riding about 25 years, but honestly I've only really been riding with knowledge for about five years, and it's made all the difference."

Katie and her husband will make the 30-hour one-way trip to Texas for Chris' Horsemanship V course. Since taking Horsemanship I, the couple have decided that clinics with their horses are more fun than cruises or a trip to Hawaii. So once a year they make the journey to Chris' ranch in Mineral Wells to take a course, and consider this their "learning vacation."

- Don't pull your horse's front end into the lead change. Push with your outside left leg and seat bone until your horse changes to the right lead. He must redistribute his weight from his now outside left hind to his now inside right hind, which he can't do if you pull his front end into the change.

- Now reverse the directions to complete a flying change from the right lead to the left.

- Take your time as you learn to change leads, and don't work on flying changes too much, or both you and your horse could become frustrated.

"Once the horse learns the relaxing cue, it becomes a reward and a 'safety zone' for him."

14

NO ROOM FOR STRESS

"Chill out! Just relax!"

Have you ever wished you could get that idea across to your horse? Well, you can. You might not be able to tell your horse to relax in so many words, but it's completely possible to teach your horse to relax on cue.

Think about a tense horse; his head usually is held high and his neck, along with the rest of his body, is rigid. He focuses on what's happening around him, not on you, his rider. Not exactly the image of the horse you want to ride into the show pen or take on a trail ride, is it?

The opposite of that tense horse is the relaxed horse with lowered head. I like to teach my horse a "relaxing cue" so that he softens his neck and drops his head on command. This is invaluable when the horse is in a potentially stressful situation, such as a

show or competition. He might be tense and start to fret because he's surrounded by strange horses, with plenty going on around him. But when I give the cue for him to relax, he quickly becomes soft, and his attention immediately comes back to me.

The relaxing cue is excellent for stressful scenarios, such as the show grounds, or any time or place your horse becomes anxious, but you also can use it in other ways for training. The cue is ideal for fine-tuning your back or getting your horse to lower his head when preparing to stop. The relaxing cue helps your horse give to the bit when you ask for collection, and keeps him soft without you relying on bit pressure. The cue can help you and your horse gain even more refinement, and you don't have to use a stronger bit to achieve it.

Whether you are into roping, cutting, reining, speed events, jumping, dressage or casual trail riding,

Teaching your horse to relax on cue is of benefit in stressful situations, as well as for training purposes.

this is a great cue to teach your horse. You'll find yourself using it many times. Once your horse learns the relaxing cue, it becomes a reward and a "safety zone" for him; it actually becomes a treat for your horse.

The Relaxing Cue

Early in your groundwork, you taught your horse to lower his head with pressure from your hand on his poll. With the relaxing cue, you teach your horse to drop his head on command while you are in the saddle. You use your feet and legs to help your horse stay soft and relaxed, and without pulling on his mouth.

To teach this cue successfully, your timing must be right on target, and your horse must clearly understand what you're asking. Don't expect to master this lesson in just one session, so take your time and, as always, end each session on a positive note.

By this point in your horse's training, he should have good vertical flexion and give vertical flexion as soon as you pick up the reins. If he doesn't, you need to go back and refine his response because vertical flexion is crucial in order to teach the relaxing cue. I've designed my entire program in a step-by-step process to make things easier on the horse. This progression of learning also helps you, the rider, but my priority has been creating a program that makes sense to the horse.

Your horse should be quiet and at ease before you start this lesson. If he tends to be energetic, ride him a bit first, because he must be calm and willing to stand still. You need all his attention focused on you.

In the beginning, use your reins and your legs together to cue the horse so that he doesn't get confused. As he starts to understand what you want, you can begin using more leg and less rein as you cue him. Eventually your horse learns to drop his head as soon as you bounce your legs against his sides, and you don't even have to use the reins.

Turn your toes in as you bump your horse's sides. Then you don't unintentionally bump with your heel and confuse him, so that he thinks he should move forward. By "bouncing" your legs, you really just slap the side of your legs against your horse's sides.

Here's how to teach your horse to respond and relax on cue.

Your horse already knows how to lower his head on cue when you're afoot. Now teach him to drop his head on command when you're in the saddle. Begin with your horse at a relaxed standstill.

Initially use your reins and legs together to cue your horse until he learns the desired response and starts to drop his head.

Gradually use more leg and less rein contact until your horse responds, ultimately, to only your leg cue.

Real People ...Real Solutions

JAMES M. LITTLEFIELD

"With the relaxing cue, no matter what we come upon while riding, I have a method to let my horse know he can relax instead of overreact."
Gus Clark

For Gus Clark, the relaxing cue has been a very practical solution. At the Boyds, Md., farm he and wife Georgie own, the couple raise Quarter Horses and Irish Sport Horses. With no fenced arena on-site, most young horse training takes place on the trail and in fields surrounding the farm. An abundance of deer in the area can lead to some rather "adventurous" situations when riding a green horse, according to Gus.

"We raised cattle for about 20 years and started raising horses in the late 1990s," said Gus. "I've worked with horses most of my life, but I didn't really have an effective program and that became obvious when we started to raise horses from birth and deal with all the issues that brings.

"I've been working with Chris during the past few years," Gus explained. "I've taken numerous clinics with him and have spent many hours under his direction. One of the invaluable techniques I learned from Chris is what he calls the relaxing cue. This technique allows me to communicate with my horse and tell him to relax on command. This cue tells him that whatever is bothering him or scaring him isn't something to worry about, and to relax his mind and body. The best part is it really works!"

It's impossible to desensitize a horse to everything he might encounter once he leaves the safety of the round pen or arena. But by following Chris' program, Gus has found that he's been able to prepare his horses – and himself – for whatever comes his way.

"With the relaxing cue, no matter what we come upon while riding, I have a method to let my horse know he can relax instead of overreact," said Gus. "What a lifesaver!"

Gus has completed Horsemanship I through III with Chris at the ranch. He continues to further his horsemanship by studying under Chris and often helps with basic instruction in Horsemanship I courses at Chris' request.

- Establish vertical flexion at a standstill.

- Turn in your toes and repeatedly bounce your legs against your horse's sides. Bounce until your horse gives by dropping his head. Some horses don't give and drop their heads right away, but others are very sensitive and catch on quickly. If your horse doesn't give, keep bouncing your legs until he does. Don't stop bouncing your legs until your horse gives; otherwise, you only confuse him. How much you must use your legs depends on the individual horse. Just continue moving your legs until your horse responds and lowers his head.

- As soon as your horse drops his head, stop bouncing your legs immediately so that he knows he's done the right thing. It's important to coordinate your cues with your horse's motions so that he understands clearly what you want. He must realize that your bouncing legs mean for him to relax and drop his head. Proceed slowly and be consistent with your cues.

- After your horse drops, then raises his head, get vertical flexion and release the reins.

- Allow your horse to stand and soak for a minute.

- Don't expect your horse to drop his head to the ground the first few times you do this exercise. Work in small increments and don't forget that crucial reward—giving relief to your horse by removing the pressure when he responds correctly.

- You are creating a habit with the relaxing cue, so just continue to ask for a little more response each time you ride. Soon, the longer you ask your horse to relax with your legs, the lower your horse's head drops. Eventually, you can ask him to hold his head just above the ground simply by giving him this relaxing cue. He should keep his head down until you pick up the reins and ask him to lift his head.

Relax and Back

As mentioned earlier, the relaxing cue is great for helping you fine-tune your horse's back. You can add refinement to both the stop and the back with this cue. Because your legs keep your horse's response soft, using the relaxing cue also allows you to stay in a snaffle bit longer without having to move to a heavier bit.

Before asking your horse to relax when he's moving, you should have the cue pol-

ished at a standstill. Be sure your horse clearly understands what that bumping with your legs means.

Now introduce the relaxing cue while your horse walks forward. He should lower his head as he walks, just as he did when standing still. If he doesn't, work with him until he understands to lower his head while moving forward—before asking him to lower his head when backing.

Some horses, especially green or inexperienced horses, hold their heads too high when backing. A horse of any age might be "sticky" or resistant to backing, and this is where the relaxing cue comes into the picture. Once

Introduce the relaxing cue as your horse walks forward before you ever ask him to relax on cue as he backs.

165

your horse gives to your cue and lowers his head, his body becomes soft and loses its resistance.

Here's how to use the relaxing cue as you back your horse.

• While centered in seat position 2 and with your horse standing still, ask your horse for vertical flexion.

• Lower your heels, exhale deeply and roll off your seat bones and onto your pockets as you sit deeply in seat position 3, just as if you're riding a Harley.

• Keep your arms straight and forward as you ask your horse to back. Your arms move backward only because your body has moved back, not because you have bent your elbows.

• If your horse resists backing or elevates his head as he backs, give the relaxing cue.

• As soon as your horse gives and lowers his head as his feet move backwards, roll forward into seat position 2 and open your hands. Don't release your hands when you are in seat position 3.

• When the back is complete, give the relaxing cue again, so your horse drops his head once more while standing still.

Relax in the Stop

Sometimes a horse tries to push against the bit when asked to stop. When this happens, I hold the reins in a brace, so I'm not pulling on his mouth and giving him something to push against. Then I give the relaxing cue and

When your horse can relax on cue, you can minimize his resistance to backing.

The relax cue also can be used to help frame your horse's body position to make a soft, smooth stop.

Real People ...Real Solutions

PRIMO MORALES PHOTOGRAPHY

"I followed Chris' advice and found that if I ask my horses for 100 percent only once in a while, they start giving it to me all the time." Rob Leach

Originally from Australia, trainer Rob Leach and Chris knew each other's families in Australia, but they met in person at a horse expo in California. When a promising futurity filly, Pep N Coda Lena, had a tough time relaxing, Rob gave Chris a call.

"The mare is pretty hot," said Rob, who trains in Hanford, Calif. "She's out of an Appendix mare, and she has a big motor. Horses can think or react, and she's so sensitive; she has a tendency to react a lot.

"Chris and I kind of come from similar backgrounds, and we rode those blood-horse types to do our jobs. If we pulled them around all the time, we didn't get much done. We had to figure out ways to slow them down to take care of business. We talked about it, and we share a very similar theory about how to ride our colts: We have to avoid training a horse while his mind is racing."

By teaching his filly to relax on cue, Rob brought about remarkable improvements. In fact, Rob and Pep N Coda Lena went on to win the limited-open championship at the 2007 Snaffle Bit Futurity.

"I work with all my horses to get them to relax and think instead of react," Rob said. "As soon as her [the filly's] mind would slow down, I could work the cow. A horse can be walking with his mind going 100 miles per

hour, or he can run with his mind going 10 miles an hour. When his feet and mind are at the same speed, that's when you can get a lot done. Getting the horse to relax and drop his head really helps."

Rob added that Chris passed along another valuable tip—realizing that you can't ask a horse for everything he's got all the time. "Not always asking your horse for 100 percent is one of the biggest things Chris taught me," Rob said.

"I see a lot of trainers asking their horses for 100 percent every day. Pretty soon that 100 percent becomes 70 percent, and then less and less, until you don't have anything left. You end up with nothing if you always ask for everything. Chris told me to back off and ask for less, and then I'd get more. Instead of being really particular and making a horse stop hard, turn hard and give everything every single time, if I started asking for less, I would start getting more. I followed Chris' advice and found that if I ask my horses for 100 percent only once in a while, they start giving it to me all the time."

Rob Leach trains reined cow horses and cutting horses, specializing in 2-year-olds. His very first Snaffle Bit Futurity was in 2007 when he won the limited-open with Pep N Coda Lena, a mare he bought for $3,000.

The goal with collection is softness, and the relaxing cue is a helpful tool to achieve that.

ask my horse to drop his head. As he does, he rounds his back and brings his hindquarters underneath his body, which is what I need for a solid stop.

"... the relaxing cue literally saves your horse's mouth."

So try using the relaxing cue to get your horse's feet "unstuck" and his body "unlocked." Then he won't push on the bit when you ask for the stop.

Relaxed Collection

Since the goal with collection is softness, the last thing I want is a horse fighting my hands or pushing against the bit. If I ask for collection and my horse doesn't immediately give it, I use the relaxing cue, bumping him with my legs so that he immediately gives and lowers his head.

This is an excellent technique for adding refinement to collection because the relaxing cue literally saves your horse's mouth. You can achieve better collection with softness and without trying different bits to acquire and maintain that softness.

"Miles on the trail go a long way toward turning a young, inexperienced horse into a thinking, working partner.... especially when you give the horse a job to do along the way."

15

HEAD DOWN THE TRAIL

Every horse—even a high-level competition horse—needs riding time away from the arena or practice area. Many riders are so consumed with perfecting maneuvers or performance that they don't take into consideration how negative constant schooling can be for the horse.

Contrary to what you might think, riding on the trail can provide an excellent physical and mental workout for both you and your horse. It would be easy to write an entire book, not just one chapter, about trail riding and the benefits it offers your horse.

Riding on the trail eliminates boredom and causes your horse to look to you for leadership. On the trail your horse also learns

Trail riding provides both horses and riders a break from routine, as well as a different atmosphere for honing their skills.

to watch where he goes and to pick up his feet. Getting out of the confines of an arena or schooling area allows you to see what your horse really knows. On the flip side, riding outside also quickly reveals any weaknesses in you and/or your horse.

> *"'Asking' gets you to only a certain point. If your horse doesn't respond to you asking him to perform, then you need to reinforce your request as necessary, always building the pressure in increments."*

I ride all my horses outside the arena once I can control them and have good forward motion. Riding outside keeps a horse from getting sour and allows me to continue teaching him in a different atmosphere. I always look for ways to keep my horse's mind busy when I'm on the trail. I want him relaxed, but always paying attention with his focus on me.

When starting a colt, some experienced riders head for open country after only a few rides in a corral. The idea is that the horse learns as he encounters different situations, so long as he has a competent rider who can stay with him. While I'd never tell a novice rider to take a green colt on the trail alone, I can testify that miles on the trail go a long way toward turning a young, inexperienced horse into a thinking, working partner, and that's especially true when the horse has a job to do along the way.

For safety's sake, make sure you and your horse have all the basic skills in place before riding on the trail. If your horse has a problem in the arena, this is magnified once you're outside the arena, so first work to master the basics in a controlled environment.

When riding a green horse, always ride with someone whose horse is quiet and steady. This also is recommended if you're nervous, even though your horse is experienced. Don't ride with someone whose horse has "issues," because you can be sure your own horse picks up on these prob-

lems. He can learn something negative just as quickly—or even more so—as he learns something positive.

Take it easy on the trail and use a series of short rides to get your horse fit and confident as you gradually build to long rides.

Before You Hit the Trail

Here are some guidelines to consider before you and your horse head down the trail.

- Know horsemanship basics and be confident of your horsemanship skills in a confined area first, before you hit the trail.

- Ride with an experienced rider on a calm, steady horse if you or your horse is nervous or inexperienced.

- Don't ride with someone whose horse has problems. Your horse can pick up on those problems, as well.

- Ride with a cell phone so you have a way to contact someone in case of an emergency on the trail. Keep the cell phone on your body, not on the saddle, in case you and your horse part ways.

- Let someone know where you're going and when you expect to be back.

- Incorporate exercises into your trail ride so your horse continues to learn.

- Build to long rides. Don't take off on a four-hour ride the first time on the trail.

Learn Along the Way

When riding along the trail, you can do plenty of exercises to improve your horsemanship and your horse's abilities. In fact, many maneuvers and exercises—in particular leg-yielding and collection—can be accomplished even more effectively outside an arena because you already have established forward motion.

First, have a plan when you trail ride. Don't head down the trail, hang on and wait for something to happen. If you wait for your horse to do something, it probably won't be what you want. Instead of waiting for your horse's feet to move first or for him to overreact on the trail, keep him busy and work with him so that his mind is on you, not his unfamiliar surroundings.

Steer and Guide

A great exercise on the trail can fine-tune the way you steer and guide your horse. Hand position plays an important role when it comes to directing your horse, and as you've learned, your horse should give in response whenever you pick up the reins.

Too often the entire time a rider is horseback, he holds onto his horse's mouth, which is a sure way to ruin the horse's sensitivity and responsiveness. Instead, you should ride with your seat and legs, and use the reins only when needed to help direct your horse. Look at it this way: You can control your horse with your seat and legs and point him in the right direction with your hands and arms. By using your reins, seat and/or legs together, you refine how you guide or steer your horse.

Recall the previous exercise, when you picked a point and rode straight to it. This exercise is easy to do on the trail and helps you work on smoothly guiding your horse.

- Pick a point, such as a tree, fence or other object, and focus on it. The point doesn't have to be in front of your horse.

- Line up your horse with the object by picking up the reins to guide his nose left or right, keeping your hands and arms forward. When you guide with the left rein, use slight right leg pressure. When you guide with the right rein, use slight left leg pressure.

- Don't overguide your horse as he moves ahead. Keep your hands forward and guide him only as needed, then release your rein pressure. Your horse should continue on a straight path unless you direct him otherwise. Don't nag at your horse's mouth by oversteering him. Constantly being in his mouth desensitizes your horse.

- Guide your horse with your reins only when he needs it. Give him the opportunity to respond correctly.

- As you travel forward, continue looking in the direction you want to go; don't look down at your horse.

- If you ride with your hands wide apart and out to the side, you encourage your horse to bend, so don't make a habit of guiding your horse this way when you want him to travel straight. Simply steer your horse in the direction you want him to go and, as soon as he goes that way, release the pressure and return to a neutral rein position.

- Another great way to fine-tune your steering is to trot figure-eights between or around trees or bushes. Doing so again reminds you to guide your horse only when necessary and to let him travel forward freely otherwise.

When on the trail, a rider all too often hangs on the horse's mouth, which is sure to ruin his sensitivity and responsiveness.

Circle a Tree

When riding on the trail or in an open field, this exercise gives your horse something practical to do, which keeps him paying attention to you, instead of just ambling along the path.

- Chose a distant tree and ride toward it. Look at the tree, not at your horse.

- As you approach the tree, use one leg in position 2 to bend your horse's ribcage so that he circles the tree with his body arced and his nose to the inside, closest to the tree. Use your leg in position 3 only if necessary because your horse needs reinforcement to bend.

- If your horse increases his speed when you haven't asked for that, use leg position 3 to move his hindquarters. "Kick him out of gear" and take away his power.

- When your horse responds softly, bending around the tree in the way you want, let him stand and soak a minute before continuing your ride.

- First, try this exercise at a walk. You also can practice circling a tree at a trot, but make a point of keeping your horse at the pace you choose; don't let your horse dictate the pace.

Controlling Speed

Some horses, especially inexperienced or young horses away from familiar surroundings, become anxious on the trail. Consciously

Circle a tree along the trail to maintain your horse's focus on you and give him something to do in this altogether different environment.

be aware of your horse in this situation. Don't allow him to jig or break into a faster gait.

If he starts to fret or becomes nervous, give him a job to do instead. Ride in serpentines or practice leg-yielding exercises so your horse's mind and body soften, and he comes back to you instead of resisting your guidance. It's very important to do these things when you first take a young horse on the trail, because you help develop his attitude for future trail riding. Habits are easily formed, so be sure they are good habits.

There's nothing more annoying on a trail ride than a horse that prances and jigs because he wants to be in the lead or tries to hurry home. Pulling back on the reins or maintaining a tight hold on the reins is what most people instinctively do. But that pulling only gives a horse something to fight, and maintaining a snug hold on the horse actually can make him worse, even more resistant to your guidance.

I've come up with a formula I call "quartering," which is effective with a horse that tends to jig or hurry anytime I ride on the trail. Instead of pulling back on the reins, I "quarter" the horse's head by pulling it 45 degrees to one side or the other. When the horse softens and brings his nose to one side, I release his head, and then pull his nose 45 degrees to the other side. This quick back-and-forth motion breaks the horse's momentum when he tries to fret or jig.

Quartering also gives the horse a release and a chance to think for himself and do the right thing. This technique also gives the horse something other than hurrying to think about. I continue quartering a fretful or jiggy horse assertively from one side to the other until the horse slows. Then I release the reins and give him the chance to travel on a loose rein. I don't mind if a horse walks fast, but if he breaks from the walk into a trot, I quarter him again, using my left hand to bring his nose to the left, and my right hand to bring his nose to the right.

This quartering is not lateral flexion; the horse's head doesn't come all the way around to my knee. When I want a horse to relax and walk, I've found that quartering is much more effective than pulling his head around fully to my knee and making him yield his hindquarters. However, if I ever am in a spot where I need to stop a horse quickly, I always can use one rein to pull his head around to my knee and stop him.

Instead of pulling on the reins to slow your horse when riding outside, "quarter" his head 45 degrees from one side to the other to break his momentum.

When your horse softens in response to quartering, release his nose and give him the opportunity to travel on a loose rein.

Practically Speaking: Be Patient with Yourself

Don't get frustrated with yourself or your horse when something goes wrong or doesn't progress as smoothly as you hoped. Instead, think of the problem as an opportunity for both you and your horse to practice and improve.

As much as everyone would like to believe it's possible, there's never a shortcut to good horsemanship. You must learn horsemanship in steps, and that takes time. So many people want a quick fix, but a quick fix doesn't hold through time. When working with horses, a weekend or weeklong course is great for giving you a sense of direction and showing you helpful techniques. But no clinic or course changes things if you don't apply what you've learned day in and day out.

You need knowledge and the willingness to hone that knowledge through time as you practice to improve your skills. There are no shortcuts. You still must walk the journey each step of the way, one day at a time.

Teach Your Horse to Stand

A common complaint I hear is about a horse that doesn't stand still for his rider. This can be frustrating and even dangerous on the trail, depending on the circumstances.

When a horse has developed this habit, again, I put him to work. A horse doesn't have to be especially bright to pick up on the idea that it takes less effort to stand still than it does to keep moving.

It always should be your idea, as the rider, to stop, to move forward or to change gaits—not your horse's idea. The following exercise is a good way to reinforce that concept if your horse needs to be reminded. Use this exercise effectively and, before long, your horse learns to take advantage of the opportunity to stand quietly and rest when you ask him to stop.

- Ask your horse to stop by using these cues: Exhale, roll back into seat position 3 and hold a brace with your arms straight, giving your horse the opportunity to stop when you correctly ask him.

- Release the reins when your horse responds and stops softly.

- If your horse stops, and then starts to move again, immediately use your leg in position 3 to push his hip and make him yield his hindquarters.

- When you take your leg off your horse's side, he should stop and stand. If he doesn't, continue to make him yield those hindquarters. Make him work until he realizes it's easier to stand quietly, rather than move around when he's asked to stop.

- Any time I think a horse is out of control, I use leg position 3 to move the horse's hip around with my leg. But if the horse wants to move forward, I back him assertively. Then I drop the reins and give him the opportunity to stand. If he again walks ahead, I back him again.

- When a horse has a lot of anxiety, I take advantage of his energy to work on other exercises I need to teach him anyway, such as leg-yielding, lateral flexion to each side, circling around a tree, backing, counter-bending or two-tracking. So I use my horse's energy to advantage by teaching him instead of trying to force him to stand still. Rather than concentrating on one exercise, I do a variety of exercises—whatever softens the horse and gives me more control. These skills also need to be developed, so I might as well work on them now, even though I do it as a form of reverse psychology. Eventually, I guarantee, the horse wants to stand quietly.

- Many horses don't want to stand quietly because they don't have the direction they need, so they don't feel comfortable. Using the exercises you've taught your horse in an arena, things he understands, helps establish security for him and builds his confidence on the trail. Asking your horse to perform these exercises gives him the leadership he needs from you. The result is a calm, confident horse, willing to stand quietly and stay there until you again ask him to move .

Crossing Water

When you confront an obstacle, it's very important that you not attempt to maneuver through it if you aren't even sure you can tackle the obstacle, or if you aren't prepared to follow through and get the job done. If you ask your horse to deal with an obstacle a couple times, but quit when he balks, as he surely will, your horse learns one thing: If he resists long enough, you give up and stop asking him to perform.

On a trail ride you never know when you might need to cross water, so it's a good idea to introduce your horse to water in a safe way. Because no horse has acute depth perception, crossing water can be especially frightening for your horse. You want to build your horse's confidence, not overwhelm him, so be that sure his first water experience is a safe one.

Know how deep the water is and that the footing isn't dangerous. A bad first water-crossing sticks with a horse and makes him apprehensive every time he encounters water in the future. Never ask your horse to cross deep water or to cross where the footing is slippery when you first teach him about dealing with water. Start in clear shallow water, where the bottom is visible; water just a few inches deep is plenty in the beginning.

Ride your horse through water, rather than leading him, as he could jump into or on top of you if he gets startled. Keep in mind: If you are nervous about crossing water, your horse picks up on that, so be calm and confident. Be persistent and consistent with your cues.

Also keep in mind that, as with every exercise, you want to set up your horse for success. Ideally, you want your horse to respond to your cues, not overreact to the situation. When a horse overreacts, he doesn't think, and your horse tends to over-react when you forcefully "tell" him what to do, instead of "asking" him to do something new or different.

This does not mean, however, that you are never firm with your horse. Start by asking kindly for what you want; then reinforce that request should your horse not respond properly. "Asking" gets you to only a certain point. If your horse doesn't respond when you ask him to perform, then you reinforce your request as necessary, always building the pressure in increments.

Here's how to approach a water-crossing with your horse.

- Ride your horse to a shallow spot in the water. Drive him forward with your legs, keep his body straight and direct his nose straight ahead so that he faces the water. If your horse doesn't have the necessary

Even if it takes several approaches to get your horse near the water, be sure and allow time for him to drop his head and smell the water.

Without the necessary impulsion, a horse might "lock up" just as he reaches the water.

Again, without the necessary impulsion, a horse might wheel to flee as he approaches the water.

The minute your horse has one or both front feet in the water, reward him by letting him relax and soak.

impulsion, you might need to use a mecate, crop or spurs, if you're effective with and experienced enough to use spurs. Use whatever method is comfortable to encourage your horse's forward movement. In such situations, many horses "lock up" and won't move forward until you urge them assertively.

• Next, let your horse put down his head to smell the water if he likes. It might take several approaches to get him this close to the water, so just reinforce your request until he is at the water.

• Now ask your horse to walk forward until he puts one or both front feet in the water. Reward him by letting him relax and soak. Ideally, he's willing to do this in the water.

• Encourage your horse to walk forward and cross the water.

• Once your horse makes an effort to cross the water, and you can tell he is trying, stop for a minute to let him relax and soak. Although the human idea of rewarding the horse might be to praise and pet him, his definition of reward is to be left alone for a minute. Be generous with this soaking time when the horse has earned it, and you can be sure it makes a positive impression on him. Letting your horse soak when he does something the right way is much more effective than drilling him and repeatedly making him do the same maneuver.

• When you succeed in crossing the water, repeat the crossing several times and in both directions. Crossing the water multiple times not only builds your horse's confidence, but the additional crossings also help him realize that it's no big deal.

• Sometimes a horse might try to lie down and roll in the water, especially if it's hot. When that happens, he usually paws the water first. If your horse does start to paw, use your legs actively to encourage him to move foward.

• Never ride with a tie-down or martingale when crossing water where your horse might have to swim. The potential for drowning a horse wearing a tie-down or martingale is tragic, but real.

After you've successfully crossed the water one time, repeat the crossing several times and in both directions until your horse is at ease.

• Later, as you introduce your horse to deeper water, you need to reward every slight try he makes, even when that's only taking another step. Don't pressure your horse so much that he loses the confidence he's gained, but let him proceed gradually.

Ride the Hills

If you want to really strengthen your horse's hindquarters, there's nothing like riding in hilly terrain. A horse needs impulsion to power up a steep hill, but sometimes a rider gets nervous and tries to hold onto the

When riding uphill, move forward into seat position 1 and keep your rein hand forward, giving your horse his head to find his way and maintain his balance.

horse's mouth. This is a mistake. The horse needs his head free so he can place his feet safely on rough, uneven ground.

When riding uphill, move forward to seat position 1 to free your horse's hindquarters and back. Be sure you don't lean too far forward, as this upsets both your balance and that of your horse. Keep your hands forward and give your horse his head. Look ahead to where you're going. Don't look down as doing so can really throw off your balance, especially on a steep uphill climb.

Move back to seat position 3 when traveling downhill, and keep your rein hand forward so you don't pull on your horse's mouth and disrupt his balance.

Ponying another horse is one approach for teaching a potentially aggressive horse to tolerate and respect a nearby horse.

When riding downhill, move back to seat position 3 with your weight in your heels. Keep your hands forward so that you don't pull on your horse's mouth, and let him pick his footing. Continue to look ahead, not down or at your horse.

It's a mistake to let a horse charge uphill or run downhill. Your horse needs momentum to go uphill, but this momentum should be controlled. If your horse tends to go too fast up- or downhill, you can use the same quartering exercise you learned earlier to break his momentum.

Quartering your horse is more effective and much safer than trying to make him yield his hindquarters on an incline because you pull only his head from side to side, and keep his body in a straight line. Be as assertive with the reins as necessary in order to be effective. Efficient rein management is critical in this situation because of the terrain.

Trail Aggression

Horses that try to kick, bite or otherwise act aggressively on the trail are more than annoying; they can be dangerous. One horse can kick at another, but break the rider's leg instead. When a horse shows aggression on

Test your horse's capacity for trail aggression by having other riders circle him, initially at a distance and then gradually coming nearer to check his reaction.

the trail, that's a clear indicator that the rider doesn't have control of his horse's mind and body; trail aggression is basically a lack of rider control.

I do not tolerate any signs of aggression, such as pinning the ears or stiffening the body to kick or bite. When a horse pins his ears, I start quartering the horse very quickly, which gives him something else to do. I don't wait until a horse actually tries to kick or bite before I assertively correct and reprimand him with my leg in position 3. The farther back along his barrel my leg is, the more sensitive the horse is. So when he gets ready to kick, I reprimand the horse.

The signs always are there before a horse reacts aggressively, so be aware of your horse. Any sign of aggression is unacceptable and should be treated as such. If your horse continues to show signs of aggression, you must raise your energy level and be even more assertive with your correction. In certain training areas you might need to become very assertive and forceful with your corrections, and this is one of those areas. Your horse must respect you, and respecting you includes him respecting other horses nearby when you ride.

Before you ever get into an actual trail-riding situation, you can test your horse and put him in a position to see if he becomes aggressive toward other horses. You don't need to wait until you are in a potentially vulnerable position on the trail to know how your horse reacts to another horse coming close by you.

I do testing in the arena by having other people ride circles close around my horse. In effect, they try to "bait" my horse into making a mistake. If he puts his ears back or shows any sign of aggression, I correct him immediately as described. My goal is to deal with any aggressive tendencies before we're on the trail.

Ponying other horses also is a good way to help your horse get over feeling aggressive when another horse is close to him. I like to introduce my horses to ponying at a young age so they learn early that they must respect other horses.

Always remember: You are responsible whenever you ride your horse. You can't get upset or blame other riders for your horse's actions. At some point everyone horseback gets into a tight space, whether in the arena or on the trail. You must be able to control your horse so that he doesn't think he can pin his ears, bite or kick others when they get too close.

"I'm big on giving a horse a purposeful job, and working with cattle does just that. Cattle work gives the horse a reason to stop, turn around, rate and think; he's learning, but he enjoys it."

16

THE CATTLE CONNECTION

Having been raised on a cattle ranch, it's only logical that I think working cattle is one of the most satisfying things to do with a horse. I could devote an entire book to cutting, roping and cattle work, but I simply want to show you how to safely introduce a horse to cattle so you can benefit from using cattle in your training routine, should you choose to do so.

I'm big on giving a horse a purposeful job, and working with cattle does just that. Cattle work gives the horse a reason to stop, turn around, rate and think; he's learning, but he enjoys it. Cattle work adds variety and interest to any training routine, and also is fun for

riders even if they never plan to compete in cattle-related events, such as cutting, working cow horse or team roping.

It takes a lot of work and training for a horse to become an accomplished cutting or reined cow horse, but you still can have fun working with cattle at a novice level. And here's the best part: Cattle work can benefit your horse, both physically and mentally.

Here at the ranch, I maintain about 200 head of Angus-cross heifers and rotate the whole group every 70 to 90 days, sending some to market and buying some fresh heifers. We rotate them because,

Whether or not you compete in the National Cutting Horse Association Futurity each year, as I do, you and your horse can benefit from using cattle in your training program.

after a time, the cattle get "used up" and sour; they get quiet and don't want to move, and we can't do much training with cattle that want to sull or stand around.

Introduce Your Horse to Cattle

If you don't have your own cattle, you might have friends with a ranch, or know someone who doesn't mind you playing horseback with his cattle. As with anything else you do with horses, you need to be smart about how you introduce your horse to cattle for the first time.

It goes without saying that you shouldn't introduce cattle into the equation if your horse doesn't already have a solid foundation. You need to have a good handle on him; he should be soft and responsive to lateral flexion, move off your legs easily, stop and turn around well. Simply put, you shouldn't wonder if you can control your horse when he meets a cow for the first time.

Sometimes a horse has never even seen a cow before, or even been close to one,

and you can't be sure how that horse might respond. If possible, try to introduce your horse to cattle, especially the first time, by riding with someone mounted on a horse that is comfortable and quiet around cattle. Doing so helps build your horse's confidence.

An entire herd can be a bit unnerving for a young horse or an inexperienced horse that has never been around cattle, so working with one cow at a time is recommended. As you would with anything potentially spooky to your horse, keep your horse facing the cow. Often the first time he sees a cow, a horse tries to spin away from the cow, so make sure you have solid control of your horse.

The easiest and safest way to introduce him to cattle is to ride behind a cow and track her around the pen, always keeping your horse's head turned toward the cow. You always want to first trail a cow, before asking your horse to get into position parallel to the cow to work it.

Trailing cattle gives your horse a reason to move along, and you quickly can tell how much handle you have with your horse. You

Take time initially to allow an inexperienced horse to become totally comfortable around cattle before asking him to sort and hold one from the herd.

Gathering the entire herd, or simply tracking only one head across the pasture, provides a great way for your horse to learn about cattle.

Practically Speaking: Importance of Good Footing

Safe footing is so important when working cattle or doing a lot of any physical activity with a horse. I'm very particular about footing and can't put too much emphasis on this. I use a sandy clay-loam mix for arena footing and in my working areas.

Footing should be soft enough and deep enough that it provides shock absorption for the horse's joints, but not too deep. Moisture—either too much of it or the lack thereof—greatly affects footing conditions. If you have questions about the footing in your working areas, I recommend consulting an expert.

want excellent control of your horse's body, with him showing plenty of suppleness and bend. Start working with cattle and any lack of body control soon becomes evident because it probably wasn't on your horse from the start.

It's good for a young horse to go outside the arena and drive or work cattle, and the experience gives me a chance to work on my techniques, as well. I like to be horseback behind cattle and drive them in a herd. This really helps a horse because his mind stays busy and focused on the cows. Tracking cattle this way also helps a horse get synchronized with the cows, and most horses soon want to start playing with the cattle. It doesn't matter whether it's a Quarter Horse, Thoroughbred, Arab or any other breed; most horses find cattle work interesting and challenging.

> "The ultimate goal is for the horse to think about the cow, not the rider, and to work on his own without you telling him what to do."

Horses are naturally superior to cattle, and the horses instinctively know this. That doesn't mean the horses don't respect cattle. Watch riders who work with rodeo livestock, and you see that their horses have developed a healthy respect for those big bucking bulls. Those horses know their jobs and get their jobs done, but every horse keeps an eye on the bulls that outweigh him by as much as 1,000 pounds.

Ability and Instruction

Many horses are bred for or have a natural ability for cattle work, but all horses must be taught. Just because your horse is bred to work cattle doesn't mean you can simply ride into a herd, drop your hand and expect him to know what to do. You must build a training foundation on your horse and put him in a position to accept the cattle, stop and turn around as he works.

If you rush your horse with cattle work, he becomes nervous and doesn't enjoy the job, and cattle work is all about building your horse's confidence and bringing out his natural instincts. With a young horse, especially, you want his mind to stay soft; you don't want him too anxious. You want him to think, not overreact, but when a horse is nervous, he tends to overreact.

Even though I want my horse to give to me and be supple, this doesn't mean I necessarily want him totally collected when I work cattle; I want him to stay natural in his work. He must be able to watch and react to the cow, not the rider, so I must position my horse to his advantage. Now the horse's priority should be the cow. My horse learns he has a job to do—controlling the cow—and the horse always should feel that he can control the situation with the cow. The more I work horses on cattle, the more I realize the horse must be comfortable and confident; otherwise, I won't achieve the results I want.

I ride all my horses in snaffles when they first start on cattle. I eventually move a horse to a short-shanked curb bit, but not until he already works well in a snaffle. Later I rotate between curb and snaffle bits, even with an advanced horse. I always go back to a snaffle, even on an older horse, just to relax him, because I've found most horses are more comfortable in a snaffle. I want a soft, slow handle on the horse before introducing a cow; in other words, he first should be comfortable and relaxed.

Prepare Your Horse to Work

When I have a horse in training on cattle, I might work him on cows five days a week, or I might work him every other day. That depends on what I'm trying to achieve.

Initially I often work a young horse at a walk and trot on a mechanical cow, so the horse starts to use his hindquarters and learns to rate the mechanical cow before I introduce a real cow. If you don't have access to a mechanical cow, you can do some exercises with your horse before you actually start any cattle work, other than just trailing them.

Be sure your horse is warmed up before working the mechanical cow or cattle, but not ridden so much that he's tired before you even get started. You want your horse softly responsive, both laterally and vertically, and paying attention to you. If he's stiff, your horse can't work a cow, so supple and bend him until he's responsive before you approach the cattle.

One exercise that I find works well in this case is to back the horse in a circle, bending his body along its arc. This helps the horse achieve more bend than walking him forward into a turnaround. I back a horse in a circle a lot, with his head to the inside of the circle, so that he moves over his hocks and bends onto

Backing with your horse's body arced in a circle is a great warm-up exercise to prepare him for working cattle.

Working a mechanical cow, if available, allows you to better control the pace while introducing your horse to cattle work.

189

Suppling exercises should be part of any routine warm-up before going to the cattle pen or pasture.

Practically Speaking: Keep it Fun

Cattle work should be enjoyable for the horse. Push your horse too much, and you end up making him anxious, frightened or resentful. Done right, cattle work helps your horse learn to think for himself and builds his confidence because you introduce a new element that adds variety and a different kind of challenge to your training routine.

Always remember that cattle work is about horsemanship and not necessarily about cutting or roping. Every horse—even one used for English disciplines—benefits from cattle work and learning to move with a cow. It gives the horse a job to do that naturally helps him use his feet and body.

the arc. His head should follow his hip. This exercise really helps the horse to back over his hocks, which is what I want, because cattle work gives my horse a reason to get on his hocks and use his hind end.

The horse also should be able to do a rollback easily and without fighting his rider. I like to "quarter" a horse back and forth here, too, by doing a rollback in one direction and then smoothly rolling back in the other direction. This encourages my horse to move off my legs and bend his rib cage. I want the horse to have good form, but be relaxed.

Attitude Adjustments

You also must pay attention to your horse's attitude. He should be responsive to you, but not scared or anxious, because if that's the case, he can't think about the cow. Your horse must be athletic and able to move well, but it's also very important that he not be worried. You want his mind relaxed so he can think and learn to read a cow.

For example, when I start a young horse on cattle, I work him on just one cow the first few times. This keeps the horse from becoming overwhelmed. Then I bring in a group of up to four older, quiet cattle and one fresh heifer. The quieter cattle, which we call the herd-settlers, help keep things easy on a young horse the first few times he works.

The ultimate goal is for your horse to think about the cow, not you, and to work on his own without you telling him what to do. You can help your horse get to this point by being there to support him, but not pushing him. You don't want to keep a snug hold of your horse's mouth, but you must be there to guide and help him with your legs and reins. You need to direct and support him, but as his confidence builds, you can let him go more. Ultimately, you're just there to help your horse get into position to work the cow.

Positioned to Work

After you have trailed cattle a few times, and your horse is comfortable with that, work him on a mechanical cow, if one is available, or start working one cow in the pen. The first cows you work individually should not be wild or skittish, as this can discourage your horse and even frighten him if he's in the wrong place at the wrong time.

Until your horse catches on to what he should do, you must help him be in the correct position to work the cow. Your horse's body should be parallel to the cow, with the horse's nose and head turned into the cow at all times so your horse's eye is cocked toward the

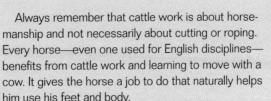

> "Don't make the mistake of dictating the turns; let your horse start thinking and reading the cow."

cow. It's important for a horse to hold a parallel line with the cow because the horse must read the cow's eyes and ears before he stops, and the horse must be able to stop before he turns. He must gather his hindquarters to roll back over his body and go the other way.

As you and your horse work, don't anticipate the cow; you don't want your horse to move before the cow moves. In this case, the cow initiates the action. Your horse does no more than the cow does. Your horse should work parallel to the cow. Then, whenever the cow stops, your horse should stop. When a cow moves, your horse should move, and when she turns, your horse should turn.

Don't make the mistake of dictating the turns to your horse; let your horse start thinking and reading the cow. Your horse soon realizes he should turn when the cow does.

*Initially work
one quiet
cow at the
time so you
can help your
horse learn
to position
himself to
maneuver
effectively.*

A horse holding a line parallel to the cow is best positioned to respond to whatever the cow does.

Despite the distance between horse and cow, the horse is able to read the cow and mirror its action.

The main things you do: Keep your horse rating the cow and teach your horse to stop before he turns.

In the turn, I help a horse a lot, using my outside leg to encourage my horse to get his hind end into the ground. But I don't want a barrel-racing turn with the horse's hind end scooting around in a circle. I want him to stop, hold the ground and follow his nose all the way through the turn and out the other side, all the while reading and rating the cow.

A common problem occurs when a horse shoulders through the turn with his head turned away from the cow, instead of his nose coming through the turn first. When shouldering through the turn, a horse doesn't have the flexibility he needs to successfully work a cow. With his shoulders out of the way, the horse's head should first follow the cow.

Unless he's balanced, your horse can't work a cow, so you want your horse "shaped up" and focused on the cow. By "shaped up," I mean that your horse's nose is toward the cow and that your horse has a slight arc in his body as he bends towards the cow. Your horse should move through a turn with his nose first, his shoulders out of the way, and his body underneath him. You want him to work over his hocks and push off his hindquarters, not his front end. When your horse has the correct body position, he can gather himself and turn quickly with a cow. The more cattle you work, the more body control you can expect from your horse. The easier and simpler you can make it on your horse, the more he enjoys his work.

In cutting competition you can't use the reins, but you can use your legs to direct your horse. Even if you never intend to compete in cutting, keep this principle in mind as you work your horse on cattle. Use your legs to help him into the correct position without confusing him by getting into his mouth too much with your hands. For example, you can use your "outside" leg opposite the cow to help push your horse's hindquarters beneath him. If you put your weight to the outside of your horse, it's easier for him to turn and go the other way.

Watching a good horse work a cow correctly should be similar to watching a dance routine—it should be smooth and stylish.

Introduce Roping

In the early stages, I use the same routine that I use with a cutting or cow horse to introduce cattle to a horse I want to use for roping.

Even if you never rope competitively, having a rope-broke horse can add another dimension to your training routine.

Your horse must be comfortable with you swinging a rope overhead before you ever cast the first loop.

First, I want a good, soft handle on the horse so I can control his body easily.

The potential roping horse also needs to be comfortable and confident, so I first trail a cow and help the horse watch and learn to read the cow. The horse needs to learn to watch and rate the cow so he can learn to be in the correct position to maneuver best.

Once the horse has a soft handle and is comfortable tracking a cow, I begin to swing a rope on my horse while trailing the cow. When I first start roping off a horse, I always use a breakaway honda. The horse must become accustomed to the feel of a cow or steer on the end of the rope, but I don't want that feel to scare my horse the first time I rope.

When you start your horse, always rope slow cattle first, so your horse can learn and his confidence can build as he starts to understand what you want him to do. Some horses seem to have a natural affinity for roping and really take to it, and you always want to respect that willingness. But even a naturally talented athlete can burn out if you ask him for too much too soon.

When you bring a horse, a rope and cattle into your riding program, you increase the risk of injury to all three parties. If you have no roping experience, it's best to learn correct techniques from a pro, avoid the typical novice mistakes and keep you and your horse as safe as possible while learning this great sport.

"For your sake and the horse's sake, don't attempt to start a young horse until you are a competent and experienced rider."

17

THE RIGHT START

Colt-starting is always one of the most popular demonstrations at horse expos and clinics. Personally, I don't think there is anything more rewarding than taking a completely green colt, starting him properly, and then progressing with him to the point he can be considered a finished horse.

Many horse owners want to learn how to start a horse, but there's a very good reason this colt-starting chapter is near the book's end instead of the beginning. Before you can safely and effectively start a green, inexperienced horse, you must be able to successfully handle and control a well-trained horse and master all of the lessons you need to tackle a young horse.

Nothing is more rewarding than starting a colt—or a more popular demonstration on my tour stops and at the horse expos.

199

Practically Speaking: Just the Basics, Please

I don't believe in using any special equipment to start a colt. I just rely on these basics:

- Rope halter with 13-foot lead rope
- Saddle pad (A blanket can flap too much.)
- Stock saddle

I do believe in using leg protection on a horse at times, but I don't put leg protection on a colt that I start. I want him to learn how to place his feet and be aware of where his feet are. I've seen horses sometimes become "immune" to this when they wear leg protection too early.

However, once I start asking a horse to perform maneuvers in which he crosses his legs, such as a turnaround, and to do things at a faster pace, I use polo wraps or boots for protection.

You must be an experienced rider to successfully start a young horse. Too many riders want to learn while they train, and most of the time the horse pays the highest price. Unfortunately, in this scenario the rider often ends up getting hurt or frustrated, as well. Some young horses need more direction than others, so you need the knowledge to provide this direction. At times you might have to change and redirect your game plan, depending on the horse's personality, and you must be an experienced rider to know when and how to do this.

For your sake and the horse's sake, don't attempt to start a young horse until you are a competent and experienced rider. An inexperienced, novice rider needs a solid, experienced horse while a young, inexperienced horse needs a solid, experienced rider.

Don't make the mistake of putting "green on green."

When to Start

When you start a colt has a lot to do with your future plans and the goals you might be

A colt must have time to think and digest what is happening so that he can learn.

trying to reach. Many futurity and racehorses actually are started under saddle in the fall of the yearling year. I prefer to wait and start all my horses when they are 2 years old. I want them to have those extra few months to mature physically and mentally.

I can do a lot with a young horse during that 2-year-old year, but I don't like to put extensive physical pressure on a horse that young. However, I can lay a very solid foundation and teach the horse a great deal without stressing his joints and bones by asking for too much too soon.

In addition to the physical aspects of training a young horse, you also must consider the mental stress it puts on a horse. Children don't start going to school for the entire day at first; instead, they start in kindergarten so they can begin learning gradually. It should be the same with young horses. They're still babies even at 2, and you need to progress step-by-step so the horse can adjust both physically and mentally to training demands. Even when you do everything the right way, stress always is involved in training.

Your Starting Mind-Set

When I work with a horse, I want to gain the horse's respect without taking away his dignity because I want the horse to keep that confidence and pride. I always try to give him choices so that being with me and working with me become his choice. This helps keep a horse fresh and keeps him thinking. After all, I don't want a robot; I want a thinking partner who looks to me for leadership. I want to set up everything so the horse wants to try his best to please me.

When you start a colt, giving him time to think and digest what you do, so he can learn, is critical at all points of the training process, but especially in the early stages. You need to be very aware of and in control of your body language, timing and rhythm so that you give the horse time to process the information he needs to perform.

Remember when you used to "cram" the night before a test at school? How much of that information that you frantically studied did you really remember a week or two later? Odds are, not much. It's the same with a colt. You can't continue to push new things at him without building his skills in steps and giving him time to accept instruction. You want to build a solid foundation

on your horse, not just get on his back and ride as soon as you can.

There is a fine line between knowing when you should continue your training session and when you should quit training your horse. You must give your horse a chance to rest and soak as he learns. If you push him too hard too fast, you lose ground, rather than progress toward your goals.

If you keep pushing your young horse until adrenaline rises and your colt goes into survival mode, he can't remember the lesson. That's why you take time to let your horse soak, and if he's breathing hard, be sure to give him a chance to catch his breath. In the end, you want your hard work and his hard work to be worth something.

I use the same theories and the same methods when starting every horse, but some horses take a more extreme application of those methods than others. With a tough horse, I sometimes have to "turn up the heat." By that I mean that I stay with my training program consistently until the young horse catches on and gives me a change in his response. If I quit before he gives this change, I defeat the whole purpose of my training.

Groundwork Preparation

People often have young horses they've bred and raised, and are excited to start training. But some young horses have been handled so much they have become disrespectful of humans. This puts anyone who begins working with that colt at a disadvantage because the young horse doesn't want to get out of the person's space.

You'll have problems with the young horse that wants to get all over you and in your space. Befriend your horse, but don't spoil him. That's a difference between a partner and a pet.

You can do a lot of preparation afoot before you ever put a saddle on a young horse. Even if he hasn't been handled much, your horse should be comfortable with a halter and know how to lead. I start my colts first in a round pen and then move to an arena. I don't use a small round pen; a 55-foot diameter is a minimum size.

Do enough groundwork with your colt that he can stand still and pay attention to you, but not so much that he's tired or bored before you saddle him. Remember: The more effective you are with your

A handler afoot or horseback can accomplish basic groundwork tasks with a colt, but either way, this is not a job for a novice.

Before ever being saddled and ridden, a colt can learn to take direction and respond to his handler.

Practically Speaking: The Value of Repetition

When I start a colt, especially one that hasn't been handled much, he has no idea what's coming next. That's one reason I do a lot of repetition, such as putting the saddle on and off numerous times. The repetition reassures the horse and lets him know there's a beginning and an end to everything I do.

If you put the saddle on a colt for the first time, cinch it down snugly and climb aboard, you just about guarantee that you'll panic the horse. He has no preparation and no clue what to expect, or what is expected of him.

My training methods are designed to continually give the horse relief and to build progressively on steps he's already learned. This keeps the horse from fretting because I constantly come back to something he's comfortable with, something he understands, and there always is a release of pressure.

Never forget how critical relief from pressure is to a horse's ability to learn and gain confidence.

groundwork, the more quickly you can accomplish these other tasks.

With your colt on the lead rope, do the basic groundwork tasks covered earlier in this book. Have your colt yield his hindquarters in both directions, and direct and drive him in both directions. Don't drill on these things, but work with him until he responds in a willing manner and yields when you ask him to give. You also want to soften your horse's rib cage before you get on him because when his body is stiff, he's more likely to buck.

You raise your colt's energy by requiring him to yield his hindquarters and by directing and driving him. When you see that his raised energy level comes down quickly, that means he's paying attention to you. You don't want your colt's energy level to stay high. You know your preparation has been effective when you can raise his energy and then watch him lower it quickly in response to whatever you ask him to do.

Once your colt yields well and pays attention with his focus on you, it's time to prepare him with the lead rope to become a riding horse. Set up each situation so your horse is prepared for and can enjoy the jobs you ask him to perform.

As you prepare your horse for the first ride, be sure you do every maneuver on both sides, or in each direction. You want the horse to think with both sides of his brain, so you need to teach him everything on both sides.

Preparation with Lead Rope

When I work a horse afoot, here's how I use my lead rope and prepare him to be ridden. I consider my lead rope an extension of my arm and use it accordingly. I want the horse to let me rub and touch all over his body and on both sides with the lead rope. If he can't accept the lead rope touching his body, there's no way he can accept the saddle. Some people call this "desensitizing" a horse, but it's really preparation.

As I rub and touch the colt, I watch the horse's body language at all times because he tells me how he's doing and when to stop what I'm doing. Watching his eyes and ears especially tells me when the colt reacts in his mind before he reacts physically and that reaction gets down to his body and feet. When I see in his eye that he's starting to react to something I've done, I stop a moment and then resume. I use rhythm and move smoothly around the colt at all times, even if I move quickly.

I never stop what I'm doing when the horse's feet are moving. If I do, that tells a colt one thing: All he has to do is move when he wants me to stop whatever I'm doing.

During this lead rope preparation, I never restrain the colt's head. The lead rope is loose and hangs over my arm at the elbow, so I can get hold of it if necessary, but where it's out of the way. As I rub and flip the rope over the colt's body, I speed up my pace, always watching to see that the colt is accepting of what I do.

After I've had the rope all over both sides of the colt's body, I bring the tail of the lead under his belly, so the rope is around his girth area, which puts some pressure there. As soon as the horse looks to me, I immediately release that slight pressure to give him relief.

I also bring the lead rope around the colt's rump on the side opposite me, but above his hocks. Then I hold steady pressure on the rope until the horse finds the relief by yielding his hindquarters and turning around to face me. As soon as he yields and begins the turn, the rope becomes slack. This helps him learn to look for relief and also to soften his body. I want the horse relaxed; if he's nervous, he isn't able to learn and give me his best.

Practically Speaking: Safe Mounting

Be sure you have a solid foundation of groundwork on your horse before you ever swing into the saddle for that first ride.

- Do your groundwork thoroughly.
- Do not mount your horse if his feet are moving. Make him yield his hindquarters until his feet stop moving, and he stands still.
- When you mount, stand at the front of his shoulder.
- Place your left hand holding the rein on the horse's neck, and make sure your horse's left eye is looking at you.
- With your right hand, twist the stirrup toward you.
- Put your toe in the stirrup and twist around until you look toward the front of your horse.
- Stand straight, distribute your weight evenly and get on the horse.
- When you dismount, place your left hand on the horse's neck. Swing your right leg over the horse until you stand beside him in the same position you had when you mounted.

The lead rope accustoms the colt to the feel of something around his belly, preparing him to later accept the cinch when he's saddled.

Bouncing up and down at a colt's shoulder helps prepare him to stand quietly when a rider mounts.

Putting weight on the colt's back prepares him to be ridden, while the continual rubbing helps maintain his comfort level and confidence.

By now, the colt is comfortable with me moving around both sides of his body and touching him all over with the lead rope. So I stand at his shoulder, facing the horse, with my left hand on his neck and my right hand on his back, and I bounce up and down beside him. This simulates the action of mounting and teaches the colt to stand quietly for that. I believe it's important to do everything on both sides, so I bounce up and down on both of the horse's sides, always watching his eyes and ears to read his mind and understand what he's thinking. Although my body moves as I bounce next to the horse, my hands are still on his back and neck.

After bouncing next to him, I then lie across the colt's back and put my weight on him. I continue rubbing him and moving around him all the time, to keep him confident of me. The horse has to realize that I'm comfortable and confident; this, in turn, builds his own level of comfort and confidence.

It's important that the horse stand still while I rub him and work with the lead rope. He should be still, with his eye on me, without restraint from the lead rope. If his feet are moving, we can't progress. A horse that doesn't stand quietly when someone afoot works around him won't stand still for mounting. During this lead rope preparation, if the horse wants to move, I use the lead rope and make him yield his hindquarters in either direction to redirect his focus back on me.

Introduce Tack

After I complete my preparation with the lead rope, I'm ready to introduce the young horse to tack.

"The more I can do with a colt on the lead rope, the more support I can offer him and the better I can give him every advantage."

First, I like to put my saddle and pad in the middle of the pen and let the horse get a good look at them. If he wants to sniff and touch my tack, that's fine. It's going to be standard equipment to him from now on, so I don't want him to feel anxious about it.

When he's comfortable around the tack, I fold the saddle pad in half and rub it all over his body, just as I did with the lead rope, always rubbing with the lay of the hair, not against it. Horses love rhythm, so I always use a steady rhythm when I work with a horse.

Then I unfold the pad and put it on the colt's back for a second before removing it. I put on and pull off the pad numerous times and on both sides, always watching the horse's eyes and ears. When I switch sides, I switch the arm I use with my lead rope. The saddle pad prepares the colt for the saddle, and the saddle is preparation for the rider, so I don't want to skip any steps. I want to pay attention to every detail, not just look ahead to the first ride.

When the colt is quiet and accepts the pad, I put the saddle on top of the pad. I always put my saddle on my hip and approach the horse at the point of his shoulder. I put the saddle on the horse for only a second or two, and then pull it off, and I do this several times and on both sides. Everything I put on the horse, I must take off him. If I never give him any relief, he'll find a way to get it. So I want to set up my horse to please me, not frustrate him.

After I've put the saddle on and taken it off a young horse several times from each side, I move the saddle around slightly on the colt's back. I want the horse to know that a saddle moving on his back is not a bad thing. Once he shows acceptance I give him a little soaking time. This is when the horse really starts to learn.

When I think the horse has accepted the saddle, I adjust the girth and fasten it loosely, just tight enough that the saddle won't come off if the horse moves. Then I immediately ask the horse to yield his hindquarters. If I can move his hind feet, there's a better chance that the horse won't buck, and I do everything I can to keep the young horse from bucking as I prepare him to be ridden.

In the past, I used to let a horse buck, but now I reprimand a horse for bucking by making him yield his hindquarters to me. With practice, afoot I've become very effective using my lead rope to get the horse to move his hindquarters. As previously described, I look at the colt's hip and use my lead rope as assertively as necessary until he yields his hind end.

A halter, saddle and pad are all that's necessary to start a colt, and he should be given ample time to investigate the equipment.

A colt must learn that every piece of equipment that's put on him can be removed; otherwise, he's anxious and never learns about that relief.

Asking a saddled colt to yield his hindquarters, and getting the job done, helps minimize the chances of bucking.

Before the first ride, directing and driving a colt around the pen helps accustom him to the feel of the saddle on his back.

As I make the horse yield his hindquarters in each direction, I gradually tighten the girth several different times. I also make some noise with the saddle, patting it and moving the stirrups.

When saddled for the first time, a lot of horses seem to think their feet are "stuck." This is why it's so important that the young horse yield those hindquarters on command. If I rush the horse, he panics, but I want him to respond to my suggestion to yield. As soon as he lifts one hind foot to yield, I release the pressure on him. I must build slowly when asking him to pick up and move his hind feet from side to side. I build on each of his responses until he successfully moves the hindquarters all the way around a circle and in each direction.

Direct and Drive

Next I move on to direct and drive the horse under saddle for the first time, but only when I can see that the horse feels "freed up" and is relaxed. Then and only then do I continue to my next step, which is to turn the colt loose in the round pen.

But I never turn a colt loose after saddling until I've handled him on the lead rope, and he responds well. I don't want him to start galloping around with no support from me. I want to be there to help him. The more I can do with a colt on the lead rope, the more support I can offer him and the better I can give him every advantage. The horse should rely on me, not his surroundings, to be comfortable.

When I do turn the horse loose, I drive the horse away from me. I want him to move out freely and get used to the saddle being on his back. Instead of letting the colt run around the pen, I "quarter" him, meaning I might let him go a quarter of the way around the pen, or circle, before I use my body language to stop the horse and turn him in the other direction Because I want the horse to relax, I don't stare directly into his eye as we work. This makes the horse uncomfortable, just as it would a person.

Here, I want to emphasize again my concerns about relying too much on a round pen. Far too often people drive horses too hard and too long in a round pen, and all this does is exhaust and frighten the horses. Overusing the pen doesn't teach the horse anything except that the handler is someone to avoid and distrust. A horse shouldn't be huffing or puffing when I get on him the first time. I don't want adrenaline to take over his system because I want him to think when I get on him, not react.

When the colt works freely in the pen, I make him move his feet, but I drive the horse with only my body language and expression until he looks at me and puts his attention on me. As soon as the horse focuses on anything other than me, I make him move again. The goal is not to wear out the horse, but to have his attention 100 percent on me. I can't proceed until I have control of his eye, and I want that eye to be soft, willing and alert. The horse should look to me for support, asking me, "What do you want me to do next?"

Once I get the horse's eye, I have his mind; when I have the mind, I can control his feet.

Again, I always notice the horse's energy level. By now, he should be able to lower his energy level quickly, which shows he isn't over-reacting to whatever I ask him to do. I like to be able to move a horse's feet to a faster pace, but then have his energy level come down quickly, with his focus on me. As the horse progresses, these transformations happen faster and faster, and that's what I look for and want.

After the loose colt totally has focused on me and has yielded in both directions to my body language, I catch him again.

The First Mounting

I don't believe in putting a bit in the horse's mouth for the first ride, so I always do the first few rides in my halter and lead rope, which is similar to riding with a bosal or hackamore.

When I think a young horse is comfortable and at ease with the saddle, I check the girth again. After checking the girth, I push and pull on the saddle a bit, so the horse experiences the sensation of the saddle moving before I get on him. Then I bounce up and down beside the horse's shoulder again, just as I did earlier. I do this on both sides of the

When first mounting a colt, maintaining eye contact with him is critical to ensure success.

As always, both sides of the horse must be introduced to any maneuver—even mounting.

A colt is less likely to give a negative response when asked to take his first step to the side, rather than straight ahead.

If a colt simply walks when he's first ridden, that's okay. This is not the time to make the horse do a lot of things.

horse with one hand steady on his neck and the other hand on the saddle, and I constantly maintain visual contact with the horse. If the horse looks away from me, that is a danger sign. I want his attention on me all the time. If I sense any unwillingness or anxiety in the horse, I go back to where the horse was last comfortable and build from that point. I never want to build on a negative response.

Many people get hurt and many horses get scared during the first mounting. So I always look at the horse's eye when I mount. That way I can read him and know that he sees me. I also make sure he stands with his feet squarely under him when I mount, and I take care that I don't accidentally put my toe in the horse's belly when mounting.

When I think the horse is ready to be ridden, I put my toe in the stirrup and hang onto the saddle for a second with my weight, and then step down again. The horse already has been prepared to accept my body weight from me lying across his back before he was saddled. I then step up and down on both sides of the horse without completely mounting until he shows acceptance.

Only then do I actually mount the horse, but I do exactly what I initially did with the saddle and pad—I get on and then get off my horse. I don't stay on him but a second or two the first couple times I mount. Again, I use that repetition.

The First Ride

After getting on and off a young horse a few times, I progressively stay on his back a little longer each time, but I never just sit still on the horse. That's the worst thing anybody can do when getting on a green horse. Instead, I rub the horse's neck and rump with my hands.

It's a mistake for me or anybody to step on a green horse, sit there and do nothing. I want the horse to know that moving is part of the equation. If I get on a horse for several days, but don't ask him to move, when I do finally ask him to move, he's most likely to explode.

I'm going to be prepared if the horse bucks, but I'm also going to do everything possible to see that he doesn't. With that in mind, I never ask him to walk forward at first. Instead, I always use the lead rope to guide him to the side and move him into a turn. The horse is much less apt to do something negative when I turn him to the side, than if I try to move him forward the first time I get on him. A lot of times when a horse is asked to go forward immediately, he either seems stuck and just stands there or he starts to buck.

When I start a colt, I don't teach him to give his head laterally before I get on him because I want him to give his hip and bend so that his body follows his nose around to the side when I pick up on the rein. So I pick up the lead rope and take my hand wide to the side to guide the horse into the turn. I use my inside leg to get his hind end moving so that he turns, and I keep rubbing him. It's very important to move that colt's hind end. As soon as his hind feet move, I release the lead rope. Then, I flip the lead rope over his nose and ask him to turn in the other direction. I continue rotating turns from side to side and asking him to move his back end in both directions multiple times before I ever ask the horse to move forward.

To ask for forward movement, I just bounce my legs on the horse's sides, but I quit asking with my legs as soon as the horse moves forward. When he starts moving, my legs stop asking. If necessary, I can turn the horse to the side and get control of his hind end. If the colt doesn't respond to my legs urging him forward, I can swing my lead rope over and under him to encourage him to move. But I keep rubbing him as he walks.

If the horse just wants to walk, that's fine. Many people get into trouble because they think they must make their horses do a lot during the first rides. If my horse breaks into a trot, or even a canter, I don't try to stop him—or to keep him going. I just let him go and ride with him. On that first ride I want to stay out of his way. And, instead of trying to stop him at first, I use a single rein to turn him to the side and move his hind end to stop him.

A lot of riders tend to be stronger going to the left, so it's important to work the horse to the right just as much. When I guide the horse's head to the side, I keep my hand down low. If my hand is high, the horse's head becomes cocked, and he starts to panic if he's suddenly off-balance. Pulling creates resistance, so I just guide the horse and avoid getting into a tug-of-war.

If the colt trots or canters, I don't try to pull him back to a walk or stop; I just relax and ride with him. And I don't pull on the saddle horn. Pulling on the horn immediately puts my body out of balance. Instead, it's

When a colt breaks into a trot, the rider taking a deep breath and relaxed attitude encourages the colt to stay relaxed and confident.

When a colt canters, it's best to relax and enjoy the ride, rather than pull on his head or the saddle horn, which can throw the young horse off balance.

better to push against the horn when there's a need to hold on. It's important to be relaxed, breathe deeply and regularly; I don't tense because the horse senses that and becomes more tense, as well.

I certainly don't use spurs on these first few rides. The horse doesn't need them, and I've found that if I use spurs when a horse is learning, he learns to push against my legs.

When I dismount, I make sure the horse is standing still. Then I step off him and walk away a few steps to give him a reward and let him realize he's done a good job.

Then I come back to the horse, pick up my lead rope and step on him again. I sit there a few seconds and dismount again. Then I untack the horse and end my first riding session on a good note.

"A young horse might be green and inexperienced, but if he trusts you and considers you the leader, you've already won half the battle."

As a horseman, it's up to me to keep the learning curve going so that my horse stays interested and happy. But that first ride doesn't need to be long at all to make it a successful one.

The Second Ride and More

Before I saddle my colt for the second ride, I always review my groundwork. I consider this troubleshooting because it helps me stay out of trouble, much like a pilot doing a pre-flight check to be sure everything works well. Even if my colt was excellent the last time I rode, I don't throw a saddle on him, step on him and go.

Everything I do on the ground has a purpose for riding. I want softness in the horse's body on the ground before I get on his back. That's where the groundwork comes into the picture, as I ask the horse to yield his hindquarters and direct and drive him.

The preparation time for the second ride and those next few rides won't take nearly as long as it did for the first ride. Preparing for the second ride should be about 50 to 65 percent faster than it took to prepare for the first ride. If I handled my groundwork and first ride correctly, I also can expect the colt to be softer today than he was yesterday. Each ride, my expectations for him should be a little greater than they were the ride before, so that he continues to progress.

On the second and subsequent rides, I still rub my horse with the saddle pad, and then I put on and take off the saddle and pad a few times before tightening my girth the first time. I always remember to tighten the girth gradually several times, not all at once. Once my horse is saddled, I again work him, asking him to yield his hindquarters and also directing and driving him in both directions. I want to take any stiffness out of his body. That's because I know whatever he does when I'm afoot, I can be sure he will try to do when I am on his back.

Because I don't want to confuse the horse at this point, I continue to use one rein at a time. Lateral control is how I take away the horse's power and also how I make him respond softly. I don't pull on both reins for several rides, probably five or six rides, or more, depending on the horse.

When I mount for the second ride, I again ask the horse to yield his hindquarters and turn to both sides at first. Then I use both legs to ask the horse to go forward. I don't make the horse do all three gaits – walk, trot and canter – but if he wants to do all three, I encourage it, and I won't pull him down to a walk or trot if he breaks into a canter on his own. If he starts going too fast, I always can bring his nose to one side and bring his hind end around in one direction or the other.

This second ride should build on the first, so I keep it short and positive for the horse. I also vary the routine so I can hold the colt's attention, and I show him my confidence through my body language.

After the first few rides, when the horse has impulsion and responds well to my legs, I tie the end of my lead rope to the halter, which makes a hackamore of sorts. By doing this, I don't have to continue throwing the lead rope over the horse's head to go in a different direction.

I always remember: My job is to never ask the horse for anything he isn't prepared to do. Most of the time when a horse gets into trouble, it's because a human has put him there by not preparing him to do the job at hand.

Subsequent rides don't have to be long to provide opportunities to develop a colt's confidence.

This colt, started during the 2007 The Road to the Horse event, negotiated a trail course soon after being ridden for the first time.

HEIDI NYLAND, COURTESY THE ROAD TO THE HORSE

Radio personality Rick Lamb (left) and The Road to the Horse producer Tootie Bailey-Bland congratulated Chris following his win at the 2007 colt-starting event. He again won the event in 2008.

I don't want to take anything for granted, no matter how quiet my horse is, and I complete each task before moving on to the next step. Most accidents happen when someone takes things for granted with a horse.

Final Thoughts on Starting Colts

Starting a young horse reveals quickly what you don't know or do correctly. Because of his inexperience, a colt isn't as forgiving as an older horse. Things can get dangerous in a hurry if you don't complete each task thoroughly before moving to the next step. Never mount a colt until you've done your homework and completed your groundwork. You only ask for trouble if you try to move ahead without finishing each step along the way. Do your preparation thoroughly and set things up for your horse to succeed, not fail.

If you aren't effective and consistent with these lessons, you need to practice on a well-trained horse before ever working with a green colt. Colt-starting isn't for everyone. A colt-starter needs to be an experienced rider who confidently can handle unexpected situations as they arise.

When a horse is nervous, you often need to do the opposite of what you might think. Instead of trying to keep a young horse still,

get him moving and give him a job to do. Raise his energy level higher than he wants it to be by making his feet move faster. Then keep his energy up until he's willing to lower it, stop and relax when you ask him to do those things. You can't force a horse to relax or stop.

Don't think you can desensitize a horse to everything he's going to encounter. Trainers do all sorts of things to a young horse in the name of desensitizing him. Personally, I think this is not only demeaning to the horse, but also totally overwhelms him. When a horse is overloaded mentally, he simply shuts down. He goes into a primitive survival mode, and at that point he doesn't learn anything. When that happens, he still can spook or blow up later, often when he's exposed to the very things you supposedly desensitized him to when he experienced the mental overload.

While you can't possibly desensitize a horse to everything in the world, you definitely can have him prepared to look to you for leadership, no matter what comes your way. When a horse is desensitized, his mind closes down and he becomes dull. I don't want my horse desensitized; I want him prepared for anything.

Always remember that forward motion and the horse's natural curiosity can take you

Practically Speaking: The Importance of Three

The number "three" seems to come up regularly when working with horses.

Through the years I've found that horses learn best in steps, and the number three often plays a role in such situations, as well.

For example, when starting a colt, I prepare him in three steps: with the lead rope, with the pad, and then with the saddle. When working a horse, I use the three rein positions: lateral left, lateral right and vertical flexion. I also use three leg positions when I ride, and describe three seat positions from front to rear in the saddle. Remember these things and be sure you use each step and each position correctly.

a long way when you start a colt. A young horse might be green and inexperienced, but if he trusts you and considers you the leader, you've already won half the battle.

If you start running into problems with your horse, never end the training session on a negative note. Finish when the horse responds positively and does something he knows—and then leave the horse alone. You might quit for the time being and pick up again later that day or wait until tomorrow. Understand that some horses simply take more time than others to learn the same lessons; that's where their individuality comes into the picture, and you must respect that and work with it.

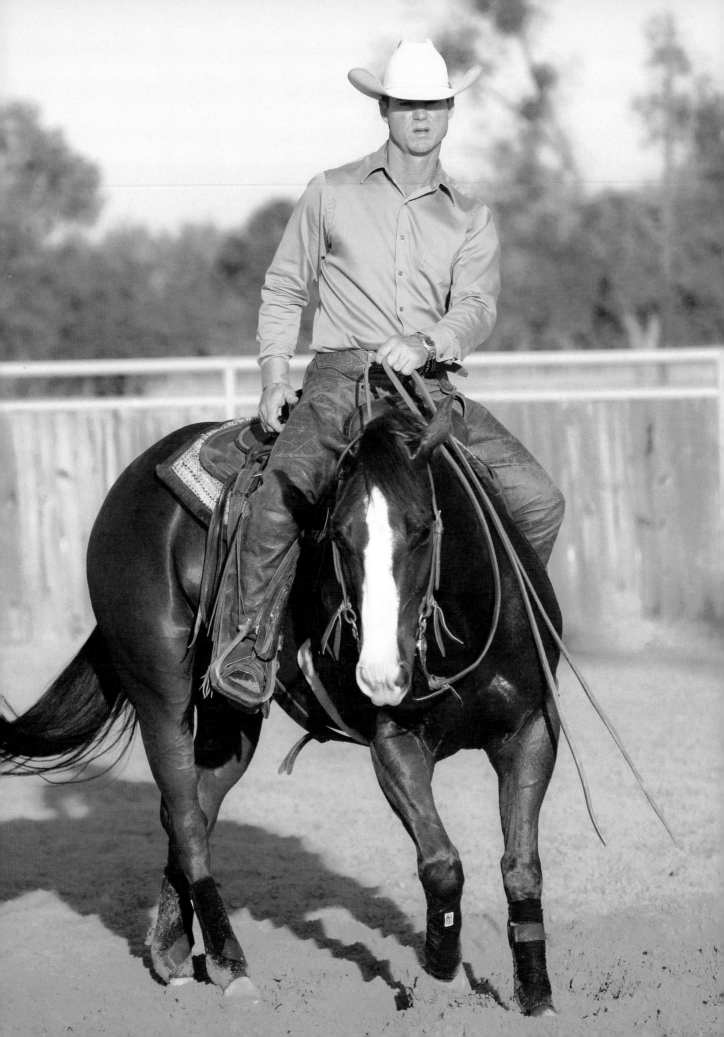

> *"The most rewarding thing to me is when my horse is happy and trying to please me."*

18
REFINE YOUR HORSEMANSHIP

To me, the most exciting thing about the journey of horsemanship is that it never ends. If you don't close your mind, you can continue to learn every single day.

Through the years, I have run into some people who believe that once you get to a certain level of horsemanship and consider yourself advanced, you're "done." You've made it. Personally, I don't think that's ever completely possible, no matter how skilled you've become. There is always more to learn; there are always more ways you can refine and cultivate your horsemanship skills.

To me, that's what horsemanship is all about. I'm constantly working on improving the methods and techniques I use in order to become a better horseman.

I'm very big on being smooth and fluid because I want my horse to be smooth and fluid, not abrupt, jumpy or coarse—either in his actions or his thoughts.

Learning to be Taught

During the last 20 years of conducting clinics, I've seen a lot of people with excuses for not learning. I believe that we have to be taught to learn, but this means being open to admitting what we don't know. I've realized that people either embrace learning or they have an excuse and ignore the facts. I've worked with many people to change their attitudes about learning, but it takes time. Most importantly, it takes willingness to learn. Once that willingness is present,

There is always more to learn, no matter how skilled the horse and rider.

When clinic students embrace learning, the changes inside ultimately are manifest outside in how each person interacts with his horse.

attitudes improve and learning escalates. The change comes from the inside of a person, but is manifest on the outside in how he deals with his horse.

You must ask yourself, "Do I really want to learn? Am I going to be insecure if someone wants to help me?"

"If you find yourself uncomfortable, it's because you've lost direction."

Our self-worth shouldn't be based on just what we know. We have to be honest with ourselves about the knowledge we really have or don't have. So many times we're guilty of thinking we have more knowledge or capability than we really have, and because of this we go too far too quickly, and this leaves gaps. If those gaps are not filled in, the foundation won't be strong and at some point, it will cave in.

Through the years, I've had to learn to become more of a "people person" and understand people more than simply understand horse training. People are a lot more complicated than horses. Horses are very natural and have many of the same qualities as people; the horses just are not as complex.

Whenever we hold a clinic orientation, we stress the importance of paying attention to details and point out how miscommunication confuses the horse when we aren't clear and effective with our direction. You, too, must be aware of and clarify the details, especially for your horse.

I think there are two basic types of learning—visualization and practical participation, and I use both when teaching clinics. To be successful, you must visualize an effective plan. The knowledge to implement that plan can be gained through learning from clinics, DVDs, articles and books. But you need to have that vision to learn effectively, which is why I stress visualization before ever attempting a task. Visualization makes you more effective when you actually do the task. You need to be able to see and feel yourself doing the task and correcting your mistakes before you make them with your horse.

Visualization is like a coach preparing the team before the game. The Australian horseman who taught me so much, Lee Reborse, told me one time, "Imagination is cheaper than experience," not to mention safer!

Whenever students come to a clinic, they bring a lot of things from their lives, including their relationships at home and at work. These things transfer directly to their horses or to the people around them in the clinic, and sometimes it takes a few days for everyone to sort through all of it.

One of the greatest satisfactions for me is seeing "the light come on" for these students and the change that comes next. They realize the change isn't because their horses are learning, but because of the acceptance and understanding that come from within the people themselves. The transformation after this realization and the progress their horses then make is remarkable.

This progress comes from being honest with yourself. Patience comes from knowledge about yourself and where you're going. You need to gain the knowledge necessary to take you to the next step so you don't get frustrated. When you're comfortable, you know where you're going with your program and your horse. If you find yourself uncomfortable, it's because you've lost direction. This carries over into everyday life as well. There is such a tie-in between your horsemanship and your relationships.

For me personally, the biggest change in my life came when I realized training my horses was not nearly as effective as training myself. This meant looking at myself in the mirror and realizing that my faults, weaknesses and insecurities showed in my horses. Once I focused on becoming a better communicator and being honest with myself, the results flowed over into my horsemanship. I'm not perfect. I still work on many things that my horses show me are my weaknesses. Horses always seek our weak areas; they know our strengths and weaknesses and show us both, and we can't just keep blaming the horses for what isn't working.

If you're really paying attention, your horse continually gives you feedback because he reacts to your movements, your cues and rhythm. When you play an instrument, but hit the wrong note, it's obvious. It's much the same with horsemanship because, if your rhythm, feel or application isn't right, a problem is going to show up in the horse. The more relaxed and in rhythm you are with your horse, the more harmony flows between the two of you, and this is apparent as you work together. As your horse feels this rhythm and flow, he can relax and be comfortable with you in the leadership role. You want your horse to listen and think so that his energy starts matching your energy. Watch a good horseman or -woman, and you honestly can't tell when the person's thoughts become the horse's thoughts because it's seamless.

I can't say enough about understanding the horse's footfall and natural balance since these are both key to refining your horsemanship. I continually work on these aspects and strive to make every transition as smooth as possible. But even more importantly, I want my horse to feel brave and confident. The most rewarding thing to me is when my horse is happy and trying to please me.

Visualization and focus are key factors in a successful riding program.

Keep Learning

Until you are confident in your abilities and have gained the experience you need, you should be working with an older horse, not a young green horse. Don't ever put yourself in a place where you don't know the next step and don't know how to follow through. Horsemanship is all about having a plan and a program.

What I enjoy most about teaching clinics at the ranch is that the people who attend are already motivated to learn, or they wouldn't be there. I appreciate the opportunity to help them develop their skills and the confidence they need to improve their lives with horses. When they leave the ranch, they're enthusiastic about what they've learned and eager to apply it. This feeling of satisfaction not only does a lot for the people attending the clinics, but it is also extremely rewarding for me. The interesting part: Every clinic is different, even if I'm teaching the same skills, because of the different personalities and issues of the people and horses involved.

I also greatly enjoy the Come Ride the Journey tours we began in 2006. These tour stops are all about motivating people to want to learn more and improve themselves. Some of these people eventually make a commit-ment to attend a course at the ranch, and I appreciate that dedication to further learning. But I have to say I really am grateful for every person who attends the tour stops and shows up for a demonstration at an expo or an event, such as The Road to the Horse.

I travel all over the world and one thing I find everywhere I go is that horsemen and -women want to learn. They're hungry for knowledge that will make them more successful with their horses. I encourage people to challenge themselves and use the program I've designed to continually refine their skills.

Add Refinement

Are you teaching your horse something every day? Are you learning something every day? If you always do the same exercises the same way, you're just going through the motions. There is a basic format to each exercise, but you can refine and advance each exercise to further your learning. Take any of the exercises you've learned in these chapters and use them as a "reality check" to gauge the progress of your horsemanship.

If you've given your horse the right foundation to build on and move forward, he's going to succeed. If that foundation isn't there, it's like asking someone to build a

Part of having a complete horsemanship program is having a good working relationship with your veterinarian.

Because of my busy tour schedule, I get to compete only once or twice a year, but one of the events I always attend is the National Cutting Horse Association Futurity.

221

two-story house and giving him only enough material for a single-story house. Your horse must fall back on instinct when he has nothing else to build on, and because the horse's instinct is all about survival, he isn't going to be thinking about you when he has to rely on instinct alone.

All the pieces we've put together to this point are part of a puzzle, part of a big picture you are continually refining. As you move on to more advanced horsemanship, all those pieces have to be in place. Rein management, natural headset, collection, leg and seat positions, moving the horse's body or head, bending his rib cage and having him move off your seat and yield to your legs, softness and suppleness—all of these are vital ingredients for fine-tuning your horsemanship.

Even when you have all the pieces in place, you're never really "done." You can still refine and improve. Any time you sense that you can be more successful at something, even if just a little bit, that tells you there is still room for improvement, still more room

for refinement. As you continue to advance your horsemanship and get results, you experience the great reward of growing into a closer partnership with your horse and getting better in increments each day.

The window for asking your horse to perform should become smaller and smaller as your horsemanship becomes more refined. In the early stages, you exaggerate your asking and your cues so your horse can clearly understand your requests. As you both progress, you begin refining these basics so that your cues become more and more subtle.

Advanced horsemanship is nothing but a refinement of the basics. Watch a classical rider performing on a high-level horse and what you witness might look like magic, but it is really just an incredible refinement of basic horsemanship skills brought together in a harmonious partnership.

Refine those Basics

After you have reached the stage where you can accomplish all of the exercises we've

No matter your preferred riding discipline, the great reward is in developing a close partnership with your horse.

Any competitive roper knows that fine-tuning proper techniques is a most effective way to achieve fast times.

The horse becomes the educator when his handler is willing to try a different approach.

covered in this book, it's time to add refinement to those exercises.

Visualize yourself and your horse performing the tasks and exercises together with more harmony. Your goal is to become so fluid and smooth that anyone watching doesn't even notice individual cues as you give them.

In the beginning your cues were obvious; they were meant to be. For example, the three leg positions are distinctly different because you initially want to make it very clear to your horse what you want from position 3 as opposed to position 1. But as your horse learns, you don't continue to exaggerate these positions, and now at this stage the difference between the three leg positions should be very slight. What once covered a large part of the horse's barrel is now reduced to mere inches. When you can bring your cues down to that and your horse still clearly knows what you are asking and responds correctly, you have refinement.

Think about how you used a "bridge" in rein management when you first learned about lateral and vertical flexion. That bridge kept your hands honest and helped you become aware of where they were at all times. But now that you are refining your rein management, you don't need to hold your reins as wide as when you directed your horse in the early stages.

Another way to add refinement is to increase the difficulty of an exercise. At this point you should be able to perform all of the tasks and exercises without using a fence to help align your horse. You also can try combining various exercises to make them more challenging. There is really no end to how you can combine these tasks to challenge yourself and your horse.

Always be aware of any stiffness in your horse's mouth, head or neck. Stiffness here is actually a result of stiffness in the body. You always want softness in your horse's mouth, as well as softness in his response to your legs. But I've found that any time a horse fights your hands, he probably also is not getting off your leg and resists with his body. If that's the case, always remember that everything on your horse works from the hind end forward. Get your horse responsive and moving off your legs, and he becomes soft and responsive in the mouth, head and neck, as well.

The more you ride with your legs and your seat, the more relaxed your horse becomes. You're riding the horse, not the saddle and not his mouth!

Forever a Student

If you make the decision to remain a student throughout your life and leave yourself open to learning, your horsemanship continues to improve. The horse becomes the educator. We're not even close to truly understanding the mind of the horse. There's still so much to learn.

The difference between a good horseman and a great horseman is passion. Commit to pursuing that passion. If we just put ourselves in a position to learn, the horse can be our greatest teacher.

PROFILE:
CYNTHIA MCFARLAND

Cynthia McFarland spent her horse-crazy childhood in Tucson, Ariz., riding mountain trails and galloping through arroyos on the back of a sorrel Quarter Horse gelding, Yuma, who was small in stature but huge in heart.

Today, Cynthia lives on a small farm outside Ocala, Fla., where she writes regularly for a number of publications, including *The Trail Rider, Horse Illustrated, Thoroughbred Times, Homestretch, The Florida Horse, Ocala Style* and others. Her writing has earned numerous awards, including a Steel Dust Award from the American Quarter Horse Association. From hands-on work in the horse industry to writing about many facets of the equine world, she has combined her lifelong passions for horses and for writing into a satisfying career

Other books Cynthia has written include *The Foaling Primer* and *The Fact Book of Horse Breeds.* She also is the author and photographer of two children's books, *Cows in the Parlor: A Visit to a Dairy Farm,* and *Hoofbeats:* The Story of a Thoroughbred.

When not busy writing, Cynthia rides the north Florida backcountry on her Paint gelding, Ben, and enjoys her other four-legged friends—cats, beef cows, and Butler, the donkey.

Books Published by WESTERN HORSEMAN®

ARABIAN LEGENDS
by Marian K. Carpenter
280 pages and 319 photographs. Abu Farwa, *Aladdinn, *Ansata Ibn Halima, *Bask, Bay-Abi, Bay El Bey, Bint Sahara, Fadjur, Ferzon, Indraff, Khemosabi, *Morafic, *Muscat, *Naborr, *Padron, *Raffles, *Raseyn, *Sakr, Samtyr, *Sanacht, *Serafix, Skorage, *Witez II, Xenophonn.

BACON & BEANS
by Stella Hughes
144 pages and 200-plus recipes for delicious Western chow.

BARREL RACING, Completely Revised
by Sharon Camarillo
128 pages, 158 photographs and 17 illustrations. Foundation horsemanship and barrel racing skills for horse and rider with additional tips on feeding, hauling and winning.

CALF ROPING
by Roy Cooper
144 pages and 280 photographs. Complete how-to coverage of roping and tying.

CHARMAYNE JAMES ON BARREL RACING
by Charmayne James with Cheryl Magoteaux
192 pages and 200-plus color photographs. Training techniques and philosophy from the most successful barrel racer in history. Vignettes that illustrate Charmayne's approach to identifying and correcting barrel-racing problems, as well as examples and experiences from her 20-plus years as a world-class competitor.

COWBOYS & BUCKAROOS
by Tim O'Byrne
176 pages and more than 250 color photograps. From an industry professional, trade secrets and the working lifestyle of these North American icons The cowboy crew's four seasons of the cattle-industry year, Cowboy and buckaroo lingo and the Cowboy Code by which they live. How they start colts, handle cattle, make long circles in rough terrain and much, much more, including excerpts from the author's personal journal offering firsthand accounts of the cowboy way.

CUTTING
by Leon Harrel
144 pages and 200 photographs. Complete guide to this popular sport involving cattle.

FIRST HORSE
by Fran Devereux Smith
176 pages, 160 black-and-white photos and numerous illustrations. Step-by-step information for the first-time horse owner and/or novice rider.

HELPFUL HINTS FOR HORSEMEN
128 pages and 325 photographs and illustrations. WH readers' and editors' tips on every facet of life with horses. Solutions to common problems horse owners share. Chapter titles: Equine Health Care; Saddles; Bits and Bridles; Gear; Knots; Trailers/Hauling Horses; Trail Riding/Backcountry Camping; Barn Equipment; Watering Systems; Pasture, Corral and Arena Equipment; Fencing and Gates; Odds and Ends.

IMPRINT TRAINING
by Robert M. Miller, D.V.M.
144 pages and 250 photographs. How to "program" newborn foals.

LEGENDARY RANCHES
By Holly endersby, Guy de Galarrd, Kathy McRaine and Tim O'Byrne
240 pages and 240 color photos. Explores the cowboys, horses, history and traditions of contemporary North American ranches. Adams, Babbitt, Bell, Crago, CS, Dragging Y, Four Sixes, Gang, Haythorn, O RO, Pitchfork, Stuart and Waggoner.

LEGENDS 1
by Diane C. Simmons with Pat Close
168 pages and 214 photographs. Barbra B, Bert, Chicaro Bill, Cowboy P-12, Depth Charge (TB), Doc Bar, Go Man Go, Hard Twist, Hollywood Gold, Joe Hancock, Joe Reed P-3, Joe Reed II, King P-234, King Fritz, Leo, Peppy, Plaudit, Poco Bueno, Poco Tivio, Queenie, Quick M Silver, Shue Fly, Star Duster, Three Bars (TB), Top Deck (TB) and Wimpy P-1.

LEGENDS 2
by Jim Goodhue, Frank Holmes, Phil Livingston and Diane C. Simmons
192 pages and 224 photographs. Clabber, Driftwood, Easy Jet, Grey Badger II, Jessie James, Jet Deck, Joe Bailey P-4 (Gonzales), Joe Bailey (Weatherford), King's Pistol, Lena's Bar, Lightning Bar, Lucky Blanton, Midnight, Midnight Jr, Moon Deck, My Texas Dandy, Oklahoma Star, Oklahoma Star Jr., Peter McCue, Rocket Bar (TB), Skipper W, Sugar Bars and Traveler.

LEGENDS 3
by Diane Ciarloni, Jim Goodhue, Kim Guenther, Frank Holmes, Betsy Lynch and Larry Thornton,
208 pages and 196 photographs. Flying Bob, Hollywood Jac 86, Jackstraw (TB), Maddon's Bright Eyes, Mr Gun Smoke, Old Sorrel, Piggin String (TB), Poco Dell, Poco Lena, Poco Pine, Question Mark, Quo Vadis, Royal King, Showdown, Steel Dust and Two Eyed Jack.

LEGENDS 4
Various Authors
216 pages and 216 photographs. Blondy's Dude, Dash For Cash, Diamonds Sparkle, Doc O'Lena, Ed Echols, Fillinic, Harlan, Impressive, Lady Bug's Moon, Miss Bank, Miss Princess/Woven Web (TB), Rebel Cause, Tonto Bars Hank, Vandy, Zan Parr Bar, Zantanon, Zippo Pine Bar.

LEGENDS 5
by Alan Gold, Sally Harrison, Frank Holmes and Ty Wyant
248 pages, approximately 300 photographs. Bartender, Bill Cody, Chicado V, Chubby, Custus Rastus (TB), Hank H, Jackie Bee, Jaguar, Joe Cody, Joe Moore, Leo San, Little Joe, Monita, Mr Bar None, Pat Star Jr., Pretty Buck, Skipa Star, and Topsail Cody.

LEGENDS 6
by Patti Campbell, Sally Harrison, Frank Holmes, GloryAnn Kurtz, Cheryl Magoteaux, Heidi Nyland, Bev Pechan and Juli S. Thorson
236 pages, approximately 270 photographs. Billietta, Caseys Charm, Colonel Freckles, Conclusive, Coy's Bonanza, Croton Oil, Doc Quixote, Doc's Prescription, Dynamic Deluxe, Flit bar, Freckles Playboy, Great Pine, Jewels Leo Bars, Major bonanza, Mr San Peppy, Okie Leo, Paul A, Peppy San, Speedy Glow and The Invester.

LEGENDS 7
by Frank Holmes, Glory Ann Kurtz, Cheryl Magoteaux, Bev Pechan, Honi Roberts, Heather S. Thomas and Juli Thorson
260 pages and 300-plus photos. Big Step, Boston Mac,

Commander King, Cutter Bill, Doc's Dee Bar, Doc's Oak, Gay Bar King, Hollywood Dun It, Jazabell Quixote, Mr Conclusion, Otoe, Peppy San Badger, Quincy Dan, Rey Jay, Rugged Lark, Skip A Barb, Sonny Dee Bar, Te N' Te, Teresa Tivio and War Leo.

NATURAL HORSE-MAN-SHIP
by Pat Parelli
224 pages and 275 photographs. Parelli's six keys to a natural horse-human relationship.

PROBLEM-SOLVING, VOLUME 1
by Marty Marten
248 pages and more than 250 photos and illustrations. How to develop a willing partnership between horse and human and improve trailer-loading, hard-to-catch, barn-sour, spooking, water-crossing, herd-bound and pull-back problems.

PROBLEM-SOLVING, VOLUME 2
by Marty Marten
231 page with photos and illustrations. A continuation of Volume 1. How-to training techniques for halter-breaking; hoof- and leg-handling, neck-reining and trail-riding problems; cinchy and head-shy horses. Sound approaches to trail riding and working cattle.

RAISE YOUR HAND IF YOU LOVE HORSES
by Pat Parelli with Kathy Swan
224 pages and 200-plus black-and-white and color photos. Autobiography of the world's foremost proponent of natural horse-manship. Pat Parelli's experiences, from the clinician's earliest remembrances to the opportunities he's enjoyed in the last decade. Bonus anecdotes from Pat's friends.

RANCH HORSEMANSHIP
by Curt Pate with Fran Devereux Smith
220 pages and more than 250 color photos and illustrations. How almost any rider at almost any level of expertise can adapt ranch-horse-training techniques to help his mount become a safer more enjoyable ride. Curt's methods to help prepare rider and horse for whatever they might encounter in the round pen, arena, pasture and beyond.

REINING, Completely Revised
by Al Dunning
216 pages and 300-plus photographs. Complete how-to training for this exciting event.

RIDE SMART
by Craig Cameron with Kathy Swan
224 pages and more than 250 black-and-white and color photos. Craig Cameron's view of horses as a species and how to develop a positive, partnering relationship with them, along with solid horsemanship skills suited for both novice and experienced riders. Ground-handling techniques, hobble-breaking methods, colt-starting, high-performance maneuvers and trailer-loading. Trouble-shooting tips and personal anecdotes about Craig's life.

RIDE THE JOURNEY
by Chris Cox with Cynthia McFarland
228 pages and 200-plus color photos. Insightful training methods from Chris Cox, 2007 and 2008 The Road to the Horse Champion. Step-by-step techniques for gaining confidence and horsemanship expertise, and for helping your equine partner reach his full potential in the arena, on the ranch or down the trail. From theory to practical application, equine psychology, natural head-set, horsemanship basics, collection and advanced maneuvers. Chapters on trail riding, starting colts and working cattle.

RODEO LEGENDS
by Gavin Ehringer
216 pages and vintage photos and life stories of rodeo greats. Joe Alexander, Jake Barnes, Joe Beaver, Leo Camarillo, Clay O'Brien Cooper, Roy Cooper, Tom Ferguson, Bruce Ford, Marvin Garrett, Don Gay, Tuff Hedeman, Charmayne James, Bill Linderman, Larry Mahan, Ty Murray, Dean Oliver, Jim Shoulders, Casey Tibbs, Harry Tompkins and Fred Whitfield.

STARTING COLTS
by Mike Kevil
168 pages and 400 photographs. Step-by-step procedure for starting colts.

THE HANK WIESCAMP STORY
by Frank Holmes
208 pages and 260-plus photographs. The biography of the legendary breeder of Quarter Horses, Appaloosas and Paints.

TEAM ROPING WITH JAKE AND CLAY
by Fran Devereux Smith
224 pages and more than 200 photographs and illustrations. Solid information for fast times from multiple world champions Jake Barnes and Clay O'Brien Cooper. Rope-handling techniques, roping dummies, and heading and heeling for practice and in competition. Sound advice about rope horses, roping steers, gear and horsemanship.

TRAIL RIDING
by Janine M. Wilder
128 pages and 150-plus color photographs. From a veteran trail rider, a comprehensive guide covering all the bases needed to enjoy this fast-growing sport. Proven methods for developing a solid trail horse, safe ways to handle various terrain, solutions for common trail problems, plus tips and resources for traveling with horses. Interesting sidebars about Janine's experiences on the trail.

WELL-SHOD
by Don Baskins
160 pages, 300 black-and-white photos and illustrations. A horse-shoeing guide for owners and farriers. Easy-to-read, step-by-step information about how to trim and shoe horses for a variety of uses. Special attention to corrective shoeing for horses with various foot and leg problems.

WIN WITH BOB AVILA
by Juli S. Thorson
Hardbound, 128 full-color pages. World champion Bob Avila's philosophies for succeeding as a competitor, breeder and trainer. The traits that separate horse-world achievers from also-rans.

WORLD CLASS REINING
by Shawn Flarida and Craig Schmersal with Kathy Swan
160 pages and 200-plus color photos. A collaboration that presents the sources' complete training program that catapulted them to reining stardom. Horse selection, training philosophies, basic foundation principles, exercises and training techniques for reining maneuvers, plus show preparation and competition strategies.

Western Horseman, established in 1936, is the world's leading horse publication. For subscription information: 800-877-5278.
To order other Western Horseman books: 800-874-6774 • Western Horseman, Box 7980, Colorado Springs, CO 80933-7980.
Web site: www.westernhorseman.com.